Character
and Conflict
in Jane Austen's
Novels

Character
and Conflict
in Jane Austen's
Novels

A PSYCHOLOGICAL APPROACH

Bernard J. Paris

Michigan State University

Wayne State University Press   Detroit, 1978

Library of Congress Cataloging in Publication Data

Paris, Bernard J
  Character and conflict in Jane Austen's novels.
  Includes biliographical references and index. 1. Austen, Jane, 1775-1817—
Characters. 2. Characters and characteristics in literature. 3. Psychology in liter-
ature. I. Title.
PR4038.C47P3   823'.7   78-13281
ISBN 0-8143-1616-6

For Susan

Contents

The novelist, we are beginning to see, has a very mixed lot of ingredients to handle. There is the story, with its time-sequence of 'and then . . . and then . . . ': there are ninepins about whom he might tell the story, and tell a rattling good one, but no, he prefers to tell his story about human beings; he takes over the life by values as well as the life in time. The characters arrive when evoked, but full of the spirit of mutiny. For they have these numerous parallels with people like ourselves, they try to live their own lives and are consequently often engaged in treason against the main scheme of the book. They 'run away,' they 'get out of hand': they are creations inside a creation, and often inharmonious towards it; if they are given complete freedom they kick the book to pieces, and if they are kept too sternly in check, they revenge themselves by dying, and destroy it by intestinal decay.

E. M. Forster, Aspects of the Novel

Preface

       The central thesis of this study is that Jane Austen's mature novels are not the models of organic unity which most critics hold them to be, but that they are beset by tensions between form, theme, and mimesis. As the first chapter will show, these tensions have several sources, the most important of which is the fact that Austen's protagonists are at once aesthetic, illustrative, and mimetic characters. They are "creations inside a creation" and, as such, are "often engaged in treason against the main scheme of the book." Since they have "numerous parallels with people like ourselves," they must be understood not only in formal and thematic, but also in motivational terms, in the same way that we understand real human beings.

  After my opening discussion of the sources of tension in Jane Austen's fiction, I shall offer formal, thematic, and psychological analyses of her four greatest novels. I shall use the theories of Northrop Frye to analyze the comic structures of Jane Austen's novels and those of Karen Horney and other Third Force psychologists to analyze her characters and her authorial personality. Frye makes only a few references to Jane Austen, but his discussion of the mythos of Spring fits her novels extremely well. The use of psychological theory will enable me to do justice to Jane Austen's mimetic achievement.

It will result in a completely new understanding of her heroines, in a greater appreciation of her genius in characterization, and in a fresh interpretation of her authorial personality. I shall conduct my thematic analyses with the conventional tools of such criticism, though my findings, I think, will often be original.

The reader will notice that I do not discuss the novels in the order of their composition. Although Elizabeth Bennet is Austen's first great mimetic character, she is one of the most difficult to understand from a psychological perspective. I have chosen to begin with Fanny Price, whose problems are more obvious. I discuss *Emma* next because it and *Mansfield Park* so beautifully complement each other. After the analyses of Fanny and Emma have been completed, it will be easier to understand the more elusive characterizations of Elizabeth and Anne.

In the final chapter, I shall reconstruct the personality which can be inferred from all of Jane Austen's writings. I shall consider her works chronologically and attempt to explain the psychodynamic process which leads her from novel to novel. There are three competing versions of Jane Austen which have emerged from the criticism. Some critics emphasize the aggressive, satirical component of her art; some stress her gentleness and conservatism; and some focus upon the detached, ironic quality of her vision. I believe that each group of critics is overemphasizing something which is there. When I analyze Jane Austen's authorial personality, I shall try to show how these diverse components of her nature are related to each other in a structure of inner conflicts.

Those who know Jane Austen criticism will be familiar with the proponents of each of the positions described above. I have chosen, for the most part, to summarize critical controversies rather than to document my agreements and disagreements with individual critics. This book has most in common with the psychological studies of Marvin Mudrick (*Jane Austen: Irony as Defense and Discovery*) and D. W. Harding ("Regulated Hatred: An Aspect of the Work of Jane Austen," *Scrutiny,* VIII [1940], 346-62), but its approach and its findings differ considerably from theirs. I am indebted to these and other critics primarily for the stimulus of their ideas, rather than for specific insights. The freshness of my interpretations will, I think, be evident. My analysis of the tensions in Jane Austen's novels and of the conflicts in her personality will at once challenge most of the existing criticism and help to make sense of the disagreements within it.

Readers who are familiar with my previous work will recognize that this book is a further application of the methodology which I developed in *A Psychological Approach to Fiction* (1974). It breaks new ground in its extended analysis of an authorial personality and in its systematic exploration of the tensions between the mythic and the mimetic poles of literature. Because of its approach, this book should interest feminist critics and students of human behavior as well as students of fiction and readers of Jane Austen. The approach can be quite helpful also to biographers who are trying to discover the author through his works and to psychohistorians (and others) who are trying to understand the relationship between the personality of an individual and the evolution of his beliefs.

The bringing together of literature and psychology can be as valuable to the student of psychology as it is to the student of literature. While discussing an aspect of vindictiveness in *Neurosis and Human Growth,* Karen Horney observed that "great writers have intuitively grasped [this phenomenon] and have presented it in more impressive forms than a psychiatrist can hope to do" (p. 198). This is true of a large number of the phenomena which psychologists have described. Psychological theory is quite reductive compared to the concrete portrayals of experience in literature. There is a reciprocal relationship, I propose, between psychological theory and the literary presentation of the phenomena which it describes. The theory provides categories of understanding which help us to recover the intuitions of the great writers about the workings of the human psyche. These intuitions, once recovered, become part of our conscious understanding of life. They amplify the theories which have helped us to perceive them and give us a phenomenological grasp of experience which cannot be gained from theory alone. The student of human behavior will be able to understand psychological phenomena in a much fuller way if he avails himself of the richness of artistic presentation.

11

I wish to thank Michigan State University for a sabbatical leave and the John Simon Guggenheim Memorial Foundation for a Fellowship which greatly facilitated the completion of this book. Typing, photocopying, and other clerical assistance have been paid for by All-University Research Grants from Michigan State University. My analysis of *Emma* first appeared in the *Psychocultural Review* and is included here, in much expanded form, with the kind permission of the editor. Portions of this study have been presented in papers given at the Conference in Modern Literature (Michigan State University, 1977) and at the Modern Language Association Convention (Chicago, 1977).

I am grateful to Howard Anderson for his encouraging response to this book as it was being written and to the graduate students who have studied Jane Austen with me for their resistance, stimulation, and consensual validation. I have been particularly stimulated by the work of George Graeber and Maggie Haselswerdt.

I am grateful to my wife, as always, for her emotional support, her astute observations, and her participation in my mental universe.

1

Form, Theme, and Mimesis

1

Jane Austen is a great comic artist, a serious interpreter of life, and a creator of brilliant mimetic characterizations. Some critics feel that she achieves, better perhaps than any other novelist, a balance between these various components of her art. But I believe that there are powerful unrecognized tensions between form, theme, and mimesis in most of Austen's novels.

These tensions are not the result of a particular weakness on her part, for they exist in almost all realistic novels and are a characteristic of the genre. As Northrop Frye observes, there are "two poles of literature," the mimetic, with its "tendency to verisimilitude and accuracy of description," and the mythic, with its "tendency to tell a story . . . about characters who can do anything."[1] Western literature has moved steadily from the mythic to the mimetic pole, generating in the process five literary modes: the mythic, the romantic, the high mimetic, the low mimetic, and the ironic. In each successive mode the power of the hero diminishes, while that of the environment increases, and wish gives way more to reality. Jane Austen's fiction belongs to the low mimetic mode in which "the hero is one of us" and we demand from the author "the same canons of probability that we find in our own experience" (*AC*, pp. 33-34). The movement toward mimesis affects only content, however. Even in the most realistic works, "we see the *same* structural principles" that we find in their pure form in myth *(AC,* p. 136). There is a built-in conflict between myth and mimesis: "the realistic writer soon finds that the requirements of literary form and plausible content always fight against each other."[2] When judged by the canons of probability, "every inherited convention of plot in literature is more or less mad."

The devices which a realistic writer uses to make his plots seem plausible and morally acceptable Frye calls "displacement." It is displacement also which accounts for the movement from mode to mode. This concept is taken from Freud, and Frye's reliance on it indicates that his system is not derived purely from an inductive survey of literature, as he claims. The conflict between the mythic and the mimetic impulses corresponds to the struggle between the pleasure principle and the reality principle, and the evolution of Western literature represents a series of stages in the development of the sense of reality. The pleasure principle is never abandoned, however, but seeks to realize itself in ways which are acceptable to the ego, which demands adaptation to reality, and to the superego, which demands conformity to a moral code. This process is especially vivid in Jane Austen, who is trying to combine comic actions with realistic characterization and serious moral concerns.

Structurally, her novels are a series of variations upon the basic "comic movement from threatening complications to a happy ending" *(AC,* p. 162). The happy ending consists in the heroine's gaining the love of a good man, the security and prestige of a desirable marriage, and the recognition of personal worth which she deserves. "The obstacles to the [heroine's] desire . . . form the action of the comedy, and the overcoming of them the comic resolution" *(AC,* p. 164). The blocking forces in

Austen's actions may be primarily internal, primarily external, or some combination of both. Elinor Dashwood, Fanny Price, and Anne Elliot have little to learn; it is a combination of unfavorable circumstances, irrational or misguided elders, and faulty social institutions or values which stands in the way of their rational desires. The main thing which they must do is to remain true to themselves, to hold onto their principles and their personal integrity in the face of external threats and disappointments. In the cases of Marianne Dashwood, Elizabeth Bennet, and Emma Woodhouse there are, to be sure, external blocking forces; but the chief obstacles to their happiness lie in themselves; and they must undergo an internal change if they are to gain their reward.

As is usual in comedy, there is a certain amount of manipulation, both in the creation and removal of blocking forces and in the final resolution of the action. "Happy endings do not impress us as true," says Frye, "but as desirable, and they are brought about by manipulation . . . . The manipulation of plot does not always involve metamorphosis of character, but there is no violation of comic decorum when it does. Unlikely conversions, miraculous transformations, and providential assistance are inseparable from comedy" (*AC,* p. 170). Since she is writing in a low mimetic mode, Austen takes some trouble to disguise the irrationalities of her plots by various devices of displacement; but she also lets us know early that we are moving in a world which is governed by the conventions of comedy; and we should not be surprised by the arbitrariness of some of her resolutions.

The fact that she is writing comedy does not interfere with Jane Austen's thematic concerns. She harmonizes form and theme by moralizing the comic action. Her satire is directed at those traits of personality, at those failures of education and judgment, and at those distortions of social customs and institutions which make daily life painful and ultimate fulfillment uncertain for good and sensitive people. The existing society at its best provides her moral norms; no happiness is possible outside of its institutions and no deviation from its values is ultimately successful. She places (in some novels, at least) a high value on individual fulfillment; but before he can be happy, a person must first be good, and her notion of goodness is strict and narrow. She employs the comic apparatus of rewards and punishments to reinforce her essentially conservative value system.

Austen's moral conservatism tends to diminish some of her comic effects. As a rule, comedy is liberal. It is on the side of desire. It celebrates the triumph of wish over reality, over all those obstacles in people, in circumstances, and in society which stand in the way of happiness. A new society crystallizes at the end; it moves, in most cases, "from a society controlled by habit, ritual bondage, arbitrary law and the older characters to a society controlled by youth and pragmatic freedom" (*AC*, p. 169). In Jane Austen's comedy there is a good deal of displacement not only in the direction of the plausible, but also in the direction of the moral. The wishes which are fulfilled in her novels are highly socialized; primitive, irrational, or selfish wishes are rarely indulged. So much has been given up, indeed, that the reader sometimes has difficulty feeling much elation at the outcome; age and sobriety seem often to triumph over youth and freedom. The heroines get what they want, but we often have trouble wanting it for them. A new society is established at the end in which rational and deserving people can be happy; but in novels like *Emma* and *Mansfield Park,* at least, not many of us would care to be in their place.

The wish fulfillment aspect of comedy seems to work best when the protagonist's "character has the neutrality which enables him to represent" desire *(AC,* p. 167), and when the ideals of the new society are relatively undefined: "We are simply given to understand that the newly-married couple will live happily ever after, or that at any rate they will get along in a relatively unhumorous and clear-sighted manner. That is one reason why the character of the successful hero is often left undeveloped: his real life begins at the end of the play, and we have to believe him to be potentially a more interesting character than he appears to be" *(AC,* p. 169). One reason why it is difficult to rejoice in Jane Austen's happy endings is that both her ideals and her protagonists are so fully developed. Our judgments must correspond closely to hers if the comic resolution is to produce its desired emotional effect; but we know so much about her values and her characters that we often find ourselves in conflict with the author, rather than under her spell. Instead of having the neutrality which allows them to represent desire, her protagonists are highly individualized human beings, often quite different from ourselves, with whom we may not readily identify.

Mimetic characterization is one of Jane Austen's most brilliant but least recognized achievements. Elizabeth Bennet, Fanny Price, Emma Woodhouse, and Anne Elliot are realistically portrayed women, each of whom is fascinating in her own right and comprehensible in terms of her own motivational system. Readers have always responded to the greatness of these characters; Austen's fiction owes much of its appeal, I am sure, to their lifelikeness and complexity. But no one seems to have understood these characters in much detail. Criticism has been focused upon their formal and thematic functions rather than upon their character structures and motivations. In order to appreciate Austen's true genius in characterization, we must approach her major figures as creations inside a creation and try to understand them as though they were real people. I have justified this practice at length in *A Psychological Approach to Fiction*, to which I must refer the reader for a full discussion,[3] but since it is still a controversial procedure, I shall recapitulate, in brief, the arguments in its favor.

There are, at present, two main schools of thought concerning characterization. Marvin Mudrick calls them the "purists" and the "realists." Characters in literature, the purists argue, are different from real people. They do not belong to the real world in which people can be understood as the products of their social and psychological histories; they belong to a fictional world in which everything they are and do is part of the author's design, part of a teleological structure whose logic is determined by formal and thematic considerations. From this point of view, as Mudrick observes, "any effort to extract them from their context and to discuss them as if they were real human beings is a sentimental misunderstanding of the nature of literature." The realists insist, however, "that characters acquire, in the course of an action, a kind of independence from the events in which they live, and that they can be usefully discussed at some distance from their context."[4] They argue that character creation can be an end in itself, that some characters are so fully realized as to have a life of their own, and that such characters can—and, indeed, should—be understood as though they were real people. Purist discussions of such characters are highly reductive. They neglect a vast amount of detail which has little formal or thematic significance, but which is there for the sake of the mimetic portrait, because the author needs it in order to represent a human being.

The purist and realist positions are not irreconcilable. In *The Nature of Narrative,* Robert Scholes and Robert Kellogg distinguish between aesthetic, illustrative, and mimetic characterization.[5] Aesthetic types exist mainly to serve technical functions or to create formal patterns and dramatic impact. Illustrative characters are most important in works with a strong allegorical or thematic interest. They are "concepts in anthropoid shape or fragments of the human psyche parading as whole human beings." We try to understand "the principle they illustrate through their actions in a narrative framework" (p. 88). Behind realistic fiction there is a strong "psychological impulse" that "tends toward the presentation of highly individualized figures who resist abstraction and generalization" (p. 101). When we encounter a fully drawn mimetic character, "we are justified in asking questions about his motivation based on our knowledge of the ways in which real people are motivated" (p. 87). What the purists say is true for aesthetic and illustrative characters, but we must employ the realist's approach if we are to appreciate mimetic characterization.

Highly developed characters often serve aesthetic, illustrative, *and* mimetic functions. When this happens, as it does with most of Jane Austen's heroines, there is usually a conflict between form, theme, and mimesis. Such characters require a combination of the purist and realist approaches: we must try to understand them both as parts of a larger structure and as persons in their own right.

As W.J. Harvey has observed in *Character and the Novel,* the purist approach has been dominant for many years.[6] One reason for this is that while we have developed sophisticated methods for analyzing many aspects of literature, we do not know how to talk about mimesis. We appreciate it, but in vague, inarticulate ways. What is required is a conceptual system congruent with the psychological phenomena which have been artistically portrayed. In *A Psychological Approach to Fiction,* I tried to show how Horneyan psychology helps us first to see and then to discuss the intricacies of much mimetic characterization. This theory works extremely well with Austen also, and I shall use it again here.[7] One particular advantage of Horneyan theory for the literary critic is that it is concerned with the strategies of defense and the structure of inner conflicts which exist in the adult. It permits us to explicate the text in a detailed way without having recourse to unconscious fantasies or childhood events for which there is no concrete evidence. The theory deals with the same psychological processes which are dramatized by the author, and it enables us to analyze the character *as given.*

When we have understood Jane Austen's characters psychologically, we shall see that the combination of mimetic characterization, comic action, and moral theme poses artistic problems which may be insoluble. Comic structure and realistic characterization involve canons of decorum, universes of discourse, which seem to be incompatible. Comic structure is highly conventional; it follows the logic of desire, and its pattern is derived, ultimately, from the mythos of Spring. Realistic characterization aims at verisimilitude; it follows the logic of motivation, of probability, of cause and effect. The reader who responds sensitively to both comic form and realistic characterization has aroused within him conflicting sets of expectations: one for the emotional satisfactions which accompany the overcoming of obstacles and the triumph of desire, the other for the pleasures of recognition which derive from verisimilitude. Realistic characters create an appetite for a consistently realistic world. We want their behavior to make sense and their fates to be commensurate with the laws of probability. Austen does not sacrifice mimetic characterization to the demands of her comic plots; her most fully realized characters remain true to their own natures up to the end. Their world, however, is often manipulated for the sake of the comic action; and when this occurs, the reader has a disturbing sense of disjunction between the demands of realism and the necessities of form. This problem would not occur if the protagonists were neutral figures or stock types who existed mainly as functions of the plot.

Realistic characterization fights against theme as well as against form. In almost all novels which attempt to combine a concrete portrayal of experience with an abstract moral perspective, a disparity arises between representation and interpretation.[8] Mimetic characters tend to escape the categories by which the author tries to understand them and to undermine his evaluation of their life styles and solutions. The great psychological realists have the capacity to see far more than they can understand. Their grasp of inner dynamics and of interpersonal relations is so subtle and profound that concrete representation is the only mode of discourse that can do it justice. When they analyze what they have represented or assign their characters illustrative roles, they are limited by the inadequacy of abstractions generally and of the conceptual systems of their day. The author's understanding of his character is often wrong and almost always oversimple. To see a mimetic character primarily through his author's eyes is to sacrifice much of his interest and complexity as a human being.

When we have understood a realistic character psychologically, we often find that our judgment, as well as our understanding, is at variance with that of the author. Novelists tend to glorify characters whose defensive strategies are similar to their own and to satirize those who have different solutions. The rhetoric of the novel and sometimes even the action are designed to gain our sympathy for the life styles and values of the approved characters. Changes from a condemned defensive strategy to an approved one are celebrated as growth and education. Insofar as the characters are mimetically portrayed, however, we are given an opportunity to understand them in our own terms and to arrive at our own judgment of their development and their solutions.

I am, of course, implying that Jane Austen celebrates unhealthy solutions. To those who go to fiction for values, this will seem a severe criticism. To me it is not. My own feeling is that though novelists do, indeed, see more than the rest of us, they are not necessarily wiser or healthier than ordinary men. We place too much value, I think, upon their attitudes and beliefs and too little upon their concrete portrayal of reality. If my experience with students is any indication, readers who find Jane Austen's morality quaint and her themes outdated will be struck by the immediacy of her novels when they understand her characters as imagined human beings. Manners change and values are debatable, but human needs and conflicts remain much the same, and mimetic truth endures.

2

Mansfield Park

1

There are a number of brilliant essays which explain "what Jane Austen meant by the creation of such a heroine" as Fanny Price.[1] The fact remains, however, that many readers cannot identify with Fanny's hopes and fears or admire her character and values in the ways that they must if the novel's comic pattern and rhetoric are to have their desired effects. Some critics complain that Fanny is insipid, others that she is a prig. The major source of difficulty, I believe, is that Fanny is a highly realized mimetic character whose human qualities are not compatible with her aesthetic and thematic roles.

The novel as a whole is designed to vindicate Fanny Price and the values for which she stands. Its highest tribute is placed in the mouth of Henry Crawford: " 'You have qualities which I had not before supposed to exist in such a degree in any human creature. You have some touches of the angel in you . . . not merely beyond what one sees . . . but beyond what one fancies might be.' " [2] If the worldly, corrupted Crawford can celebrate Fanny in such terms, we, the readers, can do no less. When we look at Fanny as a mimetic character, however, and try to understand her as a person, we see that Jane Austen is telling us, in fact, the story of a girl whose selfhood and spontaneity have been crushed by a pathogenic environment and who develops, in response, a set of socially sanctioned but personally crippling defensive strategies. No one has analyzed Fanny's psychology in detail;[3] but many readers, I am sure, have sensed the severity of her problems and have been unable to enter into Austen's glorification of her solution.

In the analysis which follows, I shall look at Fanny as an aesthetic, as an illustrative, and as a mimetic character. In exploring her aesthetic and illustrative functions, I shall be guided by the novel's rhetoric and design; I shall show what our moral, emotional, and intellectual responses are supposed to be. In understanding Fanny as a person, I shall look at Jane Austen's concrete representation of her behavior, attitudes, and experiences. The result will be a rather different Fanny from the one the author thinks she has portrayed, as well as a better appreciation of why it is difficult to respond to Fanny as Jane Austen intended.

2

Fanny is, of course, the protagonist in the comic plot. She falls in love with Edmund quite early in the novel, and much of the action centers around the creation and removal of obstacles to her desire. The chief blocking force is Edmund's love for Mary Crawford. It is removed when Mary's unprincipled response to her brother's affair with Maria reveals her true nature. Mary is charming but corrupted; Fanny is dull but good. Edmund has always appreciated Fanny's virtues, but love has blinded him to Mary's vices. The removal of his illusions saves him from a disastrous marriage and opens the way for the transfer of his affections to Fanny. He does not strike us as an exciting lover; but for Fanny he is a romantic figure, a being far above her for whom she must struggle with a rival and whose name breathes "the spirit of chivalry and warm affection" (II, iv). From Fanny's point of view, the story has an almost miraculously happy ending. She receives an "affection of which she has scarcely allowed herself to entertain a hope" (III, xvii). She is united with the hero she has always dreamed of but who has seemed unattainable.

Mansfield Park is not only about Fanny getting her wishes; it is also about Fanny getting her due. The novel is clearly a variation on the Cinderella story. Edmund appreciates Fanny's value, but everyone else treats her as personally and socially inferior. She is used as a drudge by her aunts, she is compared unfavorably with the Bertram girls and is subordinated to them, and she is excluded from the pleasures and privileges of family membership. In the course of the novel all this is reversed. Fanny becomes the favorite of Sir Thomas and Lady Bertram (replacing their disappointing daughters), she gains the love of desirable men (where her cousins have failed), and she comes to be admired as the most consistently virtuous and perceptive person around. Her chief persecutor, Aunt Norris, is appropriately punished; and she becomes one of the most valued members of the family. The happy ending brings her the full acceptance for which she has yearned and the recognition and respect which she deserves but is too modest to claim.

Fanny moves from having only one friend and many detractors to gaining the highest respect from a wide circle of admirers. Her primary enemy is Aunt Norris, who tries always to make sure that she is "lowest and last" (II, v). Her most consistent champion is Edmund, and we are invited from the outset to share his more accurate perception of her nature and his more just estimation of her worth. Fanny's shyness makes her difficult to know, but Edmund's kindness penetrates her reserve. At a time when his father thinks Fanny "far from clever" and his sisters think her "prodigiously stupid," Edmund knows her "to have a quick apprehension as well as good sense" (I, ii). He sees that she has "an affectionate heart, and a strong desire of doing right." While unsympathetic observers may scorn her as creepmouse, Edmund perceives "her to be farther entitled to attention, by great sensibility of her situation, and great timidity." The reader is supposed to identify with Edmund's attitudes of empathy, concern, and admiration and to find Fanny, as he does, "an interesting object."

Edmund is an important ally. He watches out for Fanny's health, provides for her amusement, and stands up for her rights. He gives her moral support, advice, and encouragement. His triumph over Mrs. Norris in arranging for Fanny to go to Sotherton marks the first step in Fanny's advancement toward social recognition. But as long as Mrs. Norris is such a powerful force in domestic affairs and as long as Sir Thomas is unsympathetic to Fanny, Edmund is powerless to change her overall situation. That can be done only by Sir Thomas, who is the source of all authority at Mansfield Park. In her first six years of residence Fanny makes little progress in gaining his esteem. If William comes to Mansfield, Sir Thomas tells Fanny upon his departure of Antiqua, " 'I fear he must find his sister at sixteen in some respects too much like his sister at ten' " (I, iii). Fanny "cried bitterly over this reflection." If she is to escape the persecution of Mrs. Norris and to gain the recognition which she deserves, Fanny must win the favor of her uncle.

It is the play which gives Fanny the opportunity to prove her worth. In the absence of Sir Thomas, everyone, even Edmund, goes astray. Only Fanny is beyond reproach. Edmund is quick to point this out to his father: " 'Fanny is the only one who has judged rightly throughout. . . . She never ceased to think of what was due to you. You will find Fanny everything you could wish' " (II, ii). Softened by his absence from home, attracted by Fanny's improved looks, and impressed by her virtue, Sir Thomas now takes a strong interest in Fanny; and her fortunes improve rapidly. As Fanny's star rises, Mrs. Norris's falls. Sir Thomas finds her increasingly offensive, and he effectively thwarts her efforts to exclude Fanny and to demean her. With the departure of her girl cousins, Fanny's "consequence increase[s]" further (II, iv); and, for the first time, she is invited to dinner and given a ball. She is beginning to be treated like a full-fledged member of her social world.

Fanny is no longer a despised, unappreciated, marginal figure. As the beloved of Henry Crawford she becomes, indeed, the center of attention and begins to outshine her noble cousins.

Without at all trying, Fanny has captivated a clever, proud, fastidious man, a confirmed flirt who had meant to toy with her, as he had done with others, for the gratification of his own vanity. In doing so, she triumphs over all the fashionable women who have pursued him in vain. Fanny is not conscious of her triumph; but Jane Austen makes sure, largely through Mary, that the reader appreciates it.

The conquest of Crawford is a testimony, above all, to Fanny's merit. Despite his own corruption, Henry appreciates (and wishes to appropriate) her virtues, even when he does not know them by their proper name:

> The gentleness, modesty, and sweetness of her character were warmly expatiated on. . . . Her affections were evidently strong. . . . Then, her understanding was beyond every suspicion, quick and clear; and her manners were the mirror of her own modest and elegant mind. Nor was this all. Henry Crawford had too much sense not to feel the worth of good principles in a wife, though he was too little accustomed to serious reflection to know them by their proper name; but when he talked of her having such a steadiness and regularity of conduct, such a high notion of honour, and such an observance of decorum as might warrant any man in the fullest dependence of her faith and integrity, he expressed what was inspired by the knowledge of her being well principled and religious. (II, xii)

Fanny wins not only Henry's approval, but Mary's as well: " 'There is not a better girl in the world.' " This is impressive coming from a woman like Mary, who has such "high and worldly notions of matrimony" (II, xiii). Even that misogynist the Admiral will admire Fanny: " 'for she is exactly such a woman as he thinks does not exist in the world. She is the very impossibility he would describe' " (II, xii). As we read *Mansfield Park* we sense a powerful rhetoric at work glorifying Fanny. When we look closely we find that the narrator says few things directly in her praise. There is no need to when such glowing testimonials can be put into the mouths of these worldlings.

Fanny's fortunes take a downward turn with her refusal of Henry Crawford's proposal. Sir Thomas is seriously displeased: "Self-willed, obstinate, selfish, and ungrateful. He thought her all this. She had deceived his expectations; she had lost his good opinion. What was to become of her?" (III, i). Fanny's distress is intense. Nothing—not even Edmund—is more important to her than Sir Thomas's favor and esteem. His supplying a fire in her room is a good sign, another step toward equitable treatment; but it is clear that Fanny's refusal of Crawford must be justified if Sir Thomas is to feel warmly toward her again.

Fanny's happiness seems in greatest jeopardy during her visit to Portsmouth. Sir Thomas is awaiting her change of heart, her parents do not give her the love she had hoped for, and she expects every day to hear of Edmund's marriage to Mary. She is in danger, it seems, of being left with no one to love and care for her. The noise, confusion, and confinement of her parents' home affect her health; and the author suggests that she may die if she has to endure these trials much longer (III, xi). While these aspects of her situation are arousing our anxiety for Fanny, others are working to increase her glory. Henry Crawford continues to court her, despite her low connections, and shows signs of moral growth under her influence: " 'Your judgement is my rule of right.' " The only sensible member of her family, sister Susan, regards her as an "oracle" (III, xii) and matures rapidly under her tutelage.

All of Fanny's problems are solved when Henry runs off with Maria and Julia marries Mr. Yates. With the disgrace of the Bertram girls and the downfall of Mrs. Norris, Fanny becomes the family's hope of comfort and the center of its affections. For Edmund she is " 'My Fanny—my only sister— my only comfort now' " (III, xv). Aunt Bertram is miserable until she arrives: " 'Dear Fanny! now I shall be comfortable' " (III, xvi). The behavior of Henry Crawford shows her to have been right all along, and his regret at losing her is yet another tribute to "the sweetness of her temper, the purity of her mind, and the excellence of her principles" (III, xvii). She was right about Mary as well; and when Edmund learns the truth, it is not long before he falls in love with her, thus fulfilling her fondest wish. Sir Thomas, who had feared such a marriage when he brought Fanny to Mansfield, is now overjoyed: "Fanny was indeed the daughter he wanted." Fanny's triumph is complete.

3

Thematically, *Mansfield Park* is, in a certain sense, a novel of education. It is not the heroine who is educated, however, except insofar as she is instructed by her reading and her intercourse with Edmund, who "encouraged her taste, and corrected her judgment" (II, ii). For the most part Fanny remains the same, while the people around her learn to appreciate her worth and to share her values. The most important education is that of Sir Thomas. In addition to recognizing Fanny's merit, he must see that he has been faulty as a father, mistaken about Mrs. Norris, and too worldly in his notions of marriage. In this comic action, the powerful older man is not deposed. He is an essentially good man whose faults are corrected, making him fit to lead the new society which crystallizes at the end.

Most of the characters in the novel can be placed upon a scale ranging from those who have nothing to learn at one end to those who are uneducable at the other. In the middle are the characters who are educated. At the higher end are Fanny and William Price, who are well-nigh perfect. Among the characters who learn from their experiences the range is wide. Edmund has only to be undeceived about Mary; his principles are sound. Susan is a good-natured, well-intentioned girl who excels once she learns from her sister "the obligation and expedience of submission and forebearance" (III, ix). Sir Thomas profits from his mistakes and becomes a perfect figure of authority, while Lady Bertram feels as she ought when roused by misfortune and instructed by Sir Thomas. Tom and Julia are chastened by the suffering they bring upon themselves and others and become dutiful children. Toward the lower end of the scale we find Henry and Mary Crawford. They are capable of responding to the virtues of Fanny and Edmund, but the effects of faulty training and bad companions are too strong to overcome, and they lose their chance for redemption. The uneducable characters include Mr. and Mrs. Price, who will never change, despite William's hope that Fanny will bring order and propriety into their home. Maria and Mrs. Norris are also utterly incorrigible.

There is nothing in *Mansfield Park* comparable to the complex process of change undergone by such characters as Marianne Dashwood, Elizabeth Bennet, or Emma Woodhouse. It is, however, more directly concerned than any of Jane Austen's other novels with the topic of education, with what makes people good and bad and the forces which hinder or promote their growth. Here, as elsewhere, Austen gives a good deal of importance to inherent differences—some people are sensible and some are not. But she places an even greater emphasis upon nurture. Mary Crawford has been made "delightful" by "nature": "how excellent she would have been, had she fallen into good hands earlier" (III, xvi). In Henry and Mary, in Maria, Julia, and Tom, in the unruly Price children, we see the effects of unfavorable circumstances and improper handling by the responsible adults. In Fanny, William, and Susan Price, and in Edmund Bertram, we see the result of a different sort of experience.

The contrast, quite simply, is between spoiled and unspoiled children. Children turn out well or ill according to the degree that they have been privileged and indulged. Spoiled children are selfish, proud, and rebellious; unspoiled children are unselfish, humble, and submissive to authority. Spoiled children are idle; unspoiled children work. Spoiled children lack morals and propriety; unspoiled children are principled and correct. Spoiled children love the light and lively; unspoiled children are sober and steady. Spoiled children are restless and unsatisfied; unspoiled children are tranquil and content. If a child has not been too severely spoiled and does not lack sense, he can be cured by suffering and good example. Suffering is efficacious in some older people too. Lady Bertram is roused to true feeling by Tom's illness and to moral awareness by Maria's behavior. The changes in Sir Thomas are brought about largely by his sufferings, first in Antigua and then over his failures and disappointments as a father.

Reflecting on Fanny, William, and Susan Price, Sir Thomas sees "repeated reason to . . . acknowledge the advantage of early hardship and discipline, and the consciousness of being born to struggle and endure" (III, xvii). His own daughters, he

29

recognizes, "had never been properly taught to govern their inclinations and tempers, by that sense of duty which can alone suffice." Born to privilege and spoiled by Mrs. Norris, they have not learned "the necessity of self-denial and humility." Julia "escape[s] better than Maria" because she has "been less the darling of [Mrs. Norris], less flattered and less spoilt. Her beauty and acquirements had held but a second place . . . education had not given her so very hurtful a degree of self-consequence." As a result she "submitted the best to the disappointment in Henry Crawford"; and though she makes a hasty and ill-advised marriage, she returns home "humble and wishing to be forgiven."

Though Jane Austen does not stress the point, Edmund's goodness has something to do with his being a younger son. This in itself is a "hardship and discipline"; he must struggle to make a place for himself in the world and endure his subordination to a less worthy brother. Tom has "no want of sense" and good examples at home, but his privileged position and the companions and pursuits to which it leads him induce "habits" of "thoughtlessness and selfishness" which bring evils to his family and serious illness to himself. As a result of his illness, Tom suffers and learns to think. The "self- reproach" arising from Maria's downfall, "to which he felt himself accessary by all the dangerous intimacy of his unjustifiable theatre" makes a permanent impression upon his mind: "He became what he ought to be, useful to his father, steady and quiet, and not living merely for himself" (III, xvii).

Henry Crawford is also well endowed (otherwise neither Edmund nor Sir Thomas would be so deceived); but, like Tom, he becomes "thoughtless and selfish from prosperity and bad example" (I, xii). The bad example in his case is a figure of authority, the Admiral, who sets the tone for Henry's dealings with women. Henry is "ruined by early independence" (III, xvii). Before his majority the Admiral lets him have his way far more than a father would (II, xii); and when he comes into his estate he has the wealth and power to do what he wishes, without ever having learned responsibility. Given these conditions, it is no wonder that he is vain, unsteady, and self-indulgent. His admiration for Fanny shows that he still has a moral sense, but it is too undeveloped to save him from temptation. Henry is contrasted with William Price. The same vague sense of his own deficiencies which leads him to worship Fanny makes him, for a fleeting moment, at least, envy and admire William: "The glory of heroism, of usefulness, of exertion, of endurance, made his own habits of selfish indulgence appear in shameful contrast; and he wished he had been a William Price . . . working his way to fortune and consequence with so much self-respect and happy ardour, instead of what he was!" (II, vi).

William is a favorite child, but the partiality of his mother is counterbalanced, evidently, by the hardship of his lot, the necessity to struggle and endure. On her return to Portsmouth, Fanny cannot help but see that her mother is "a partial, ill-judging parent . . . who neither taught nor restrained her children" (III, viii). As a consequence, her children are uncivilized; and her home is "the abode of noise, disorder, and impropriety." It is the opposite of Mansfield Park, which, under the rational authority of the enlightened Sir Thomas, has become the symbol of a justly ordered society in which everyone is in his right place and everything is done as it ought to be. In her uncle's house, thinks Fanny, "there would have been a consideration of times and seasons, a regulation of subject, a propriety, an attention towards every body which there was not here" (III, vii). Attention is unevenly divided in the Price household. Toward her sons and her daughter Betsey Mrs. Price is "most injudiciously indulgent" (III, viii). Susan, who has taken over Fanny's place in the family, has never known "the blind fondness which was for ever producing evil around her" (III, ix). As we might expect, it is Susan who is the good child. She tries to create a better order in her home, but finds that it is fruitless to contend with an irrational authority. She profits from Fanny's lessons on submission and forebearance and flourishes when transplanted to the well-ordered world of Mansfield Park.

It is Fanny, of course, who best supports the theory of education which is being advanced in this novel. She has suffered the most from "early hardship and discipline, and the consciousness of being born to struggle and endure"; and she turns out to be the ideal woman, wife, and daughter. She has a nervous temperament, to be sure, from which Susan is happily free; but as a moral being she has "some touches of the angel" and is almost beyond praise.

4

I have been examining certain aspects of the aesthetic and thematic structures of *Mansfield Park* with the object of understanding how Jane Austen meant us to think and feel about Fanny Price. I contended at the outset that Fanny is a highly realized mimetic character, a creation inside a creation, whose human qualities are not compatible with her aesthetic and thematic roles. When we understand Fanny psychologically, it is difficult to regard her as the angelic being she is supposed to be and to accept the powerful rhetoric which aims at her glorification. We may be at odds with the author also in our response to the education theme. Jane Austen seems perceptive enough in her criticism of the spoiled children, but it is difficult to agree with her celebration of hardship, struggle, and suffering and the effects which they produce.

Part of the problem is that the author herself has invited our indignation at the way in which Fanny has been treated. Her "motives [have] often been misunderstood, her feelings disregarded, and her comprehension under-valued; . . . she [has] known the pains of tyranny, of ridicule, and neglect" (I, xvi). It is difficult, suddenly, to regard this " 'abominable . . . unkindness' " (II, xii) as advantageous. An even greater obstacle to our acceptance of the author's final view of Fanny's education is that she shows us, in her concrete portrayal of Fanny, how destructive this awful treatment has been. For reasons of her own, Jane Austen needed to glorify suffering and to believe that struggle and privation make one a better person. This did not prevent her from portraying quite accurately, however, the crippling effects of Fanny's childhood upon her personality. When we see Fanny as a person, it is hard to believe that the bad treatment she received was good for her and that she turned out well. She is as damaged as the spoiled children, but in a different way.

We do not sympathize with Fanny as much or find her as interesting as we might because Austen asks us to admire her. But when we look at Fanny as a person, rather than as a heroine, our compassionate feelings are liberated and we find her to be a complex and fascinating psychological portrait. In order to appreciate fully the intricacies of her character and the greatness of Austen's mimetic achievement, we need to look at Fanny from the perspective of an appropriate psychological theory. Those who are familiar with my use of Third Force psychology in the study of literary characters may already have seen that Fanny is a remarkable example of Karen Horney's self-effacing personality. For the benefit of those who are unfamiliar with Third Force psychology, I shall present here a brief account of its theories. Some of the material applies directly to *Mansfield Park;* some of it will not be used until we deal with other novels.[4]

Third Force psychologists see healthy human development as a process of self-actualization and unhealthy development as a process of self-alienation. They contend, in essence, that man is not simply a tension-reducing or a conditioned animal, but that there is present in him a third force, an "evolutionary constructive" force, which urges "him to realize his given potentialities."[5] Each man has "an essential biologically based inner nature" which is "good or neutral rather than bad" and which should be brought out and encouraged rather than suppressed. If this inner nature "is permitted to guide our life, we grow healthy, fruitful, and happy." If it is "denied or suppressed," we get sick. This inner nature "is weak and delicate and subtle and easily overcome by habit, cultural pressure, and wrong attitudes toward it."[6]

One of the most interesting Third Force contributions to our understanding of man's essential nature is Abraham Maslow's theory of the hierarchy of basic needs. According to this theory, all men have needs for physiological satisfaction, for safety, for love and belonging, for self-esteem, and for self-actualization.[7] These needs are not always experienced consciously; indeed, they tend to be more unconscious than conscious. They are hierarchical in that they exist in an order of prepotency; the physiological needs are the most powerful, and so on. The needs at the upper end of the hierarchy are much weaker than the lower needs, though they are no less basic. All of the needs are basic in the sense that they are built into man's nature as a function of his biological structure, and they must be gratified if the organism is to develop in a healthy way.

Each individual presses by nature for the fulfillment of all these needs, but at any given time his motivational life will be centered around the fulfillment of one of the needs. Since a higher need emerges strongly only when the needs below it have been sufficiently met, the individual tends to be occupied with the basic needs in the order of their prepotency. The person living in an environment which is favorable to growth will move steadily up the hierarchy until he is free to devote most of his energies to self-actualization; this is the full and satisfying use of his capacities in a calling which suits his nature.

The hierarchy of basic needs, then, establishes the pattern of psychological evolution. If the individual is not adequately fulfilled in his lower needs, he may become fixated at an early state of development; or, if he passes beyond, he may be subject to frequent regressions. Frustration of a basic need intensifies it and insures its persistence, whereas gratification diminishes its strength as a motivating force. Gratification of the basic needs produces health; it permits the individual to continue on his way toward self-actualization. Frustration of the basic needs produces pathology; it arrests the individual's development, alienates him from his real self, and leads him to develop neurotic strategies for making up his deficiencies.

The concept of the real self is the foundation of both Maslow's and Horney's systems. Under favorable conditions, says Horney, the individual "will develop . . . the unique alive forces of his real self: the clarity and depth of his own feelings, thoughts, wishes, interests; the ability to tap his own resources, the strength of his will power; the special capacities or gifts he may have; the faculty to express himself, and to relate himself to others with his spontaneous feelings. All this will in time enable him to find his set of values and his aims in life" *(NHG,*

p. 17). The real self is not very strong, however, and it is frequently abandoned. The child is a weak and dependent being whose needs for safety, love, and acceptance are so strong that he will sacrifice himself, if necessary, in order to get these things. "The primal choice," says Maslow, "is between others and one's own self. If the only way to maintain the self is to lose the other, then the ordinary child will give up the self" (*PB*, p. 50).

The person who is able to develop in accordance with his real self possesses a number of characteristics which distinguish him from the self-alienated person. The child who is not permitted to be himself and who does not live in a safe, relatively transparent world develops a defensiveness which cuts him off both from himself and from external reality. The opposite of defensiveness is "openness to experience," and the self-actualizing person is characterized above all by his openness to his own inner being and to the world around him.

The self-actualizing person's openness to himself is manifested in his greater congruence, his greater transparence, and his greater spontaneity. A person is congruent, says Carl Rogers, when whatever feeling or attitude he is experiencing is matched by his awareness of that attitude.[8] He is not self-deceived or torn by unconscious conflicts. A person is transparent when his acts, words, and gestures accurately indicate what is going on inside of him. Transparency requires self-acceptance and a confidence that one's real self will be accepted by other people or that one can handle rejection. Spontaneity involves an absence of inhibition both in experiencing and in expressing the real self. It cannot exist without a profound trust both in self and others.

The self-actualizing person is distinguished not only by his courage to be himself, but also by his courage to be in the world. Ernest Schachtel sees human development as, in part, a conflict between our tendencies toward embeddedness and our tendencies toward openness and growth. There is in every man's psychic evolution "a conflict between the wish to remain embedded in the womb or in the mother's care, eventually in the accustomed, the fear of separation from such embeddedness, and the wish to encounter the world and to develop and realize, in this encounter, the human capacities."[9] In the course of healthy development, "the embeddedness principle yields to the transcendence principle of openness toward the world and of self-realization which takes place in the encounter with the world" *(M,* p. 157). Under unfavorable conditions, such as "anxiety-arousing early experiences in the child-parent relationship, the embeddedness principle may remain pathologically strong, with the result that the encounter with the world is experienced in an autocentric way as an unwelcome impinging of disturbing stimuli" *(M,* pp. 157-158). When this happens, the individual fears and avoids "everything new or strange that might disturb the . . . embeddedness in a closed pattern or routine, which may be the pattern of a particular culture, a particular social group, a personal routine pattern of life, or usually, a combination of all these" *(M,* p. 167). Embeddedness and openness are always matters of degree; the conflict between them is never finally resolved: "Man always lives somewhere between these two poles of clinging to a rigid attitude with its closed world and of leaping into the stream of life with his senses open toward the inexhaustible, changing, infinite world" *(M,* pp. 199-200).

Frustration of the basic needs produces a number of defensive strategies, all of which cut us off from ourselves and from the world and intensify our tendencies toward embeddedness. A brilliant analysis of these strategies can be found in Karen Horney's work, particularly in her last book, *Neurosis and Human Growth.* Before we discuss Horney, however, let us look at Fanny Price from the perspective of the theories which have been presented so far.

Fanny is the product of a pathogenic environment which forces her to develop in a self-alienated way. She does not feel safe, she does not feel loved and accepted, and she has little self-esteem. She is severely deprived of the external support which she needs in order to grow. She receives reinforcement from William and Edmund; but it is not enough to counterbalance the absence of parental love, a secure home, respect for her needs, and fair treatment. "Apprehensiveness, fear, dread and anxiety, tension, nervousness, and jitteriness are all consequences of safety-need frustration" *(MP,* p. 144); and Fanny displays all of these characteristics. She perceives the world "to be hostile, overwhelming, and threatening"; she "behaves as if a great catastrophe were almost always impending"; and she is engaged "in a search for a protector" *(MP,* p. 88). She becomes "the quiet, . . . serving, dependent person" who is the product of insecurity and low self-esteem *(MP,* p. 53).

Self-actualization is never an issue, either for Fanny or for the author. Constitutionally feeble to begin with, Fanny has no chance to be her own person in the chaotic, competitive, unsympathetic milieu of the Price household. She subordinates herself entirely to others in the hope of gaining some scrap of love, praise, consequence, and protection. What is at issue is not whether Fanny will be able to grow, but whether her self-sacrifice will be appreciated. Since Jane Austen is highly sympathetic to Fanny's solution, she makes it work. By the end Fanny receives in abundant supply the love, security, and recognition of which she had been so severely deprived. This calms her nerves, and she becomes less anxious than she had been. But her ways are set; her development has been arrested. Her circumstances are much better, but there is no evidence that this produces inner liberation. Fanny's lack of spontaneity does not bother Jane Austen because she approves the rigidities which deprivation has produced in her heroine.

In Rogers' terms, Fanny completely lacks congruence, transparence, and spontaneity. As we shall see, her defense system is such that she cannot permit herself to feel resentment, envy, or triumph. As a result, she represses these feelings or feels them on behalf of someone else. On other occasions, she consciously experiences feelings which she is supposed to have but which are at odds with her deepest attitudes, as when she reproaches herself for her "want of attention" to poor, lonely Aunt Norris, whom she hates (II, xi). Her friendly or concerned feelings toward her girl cousins seem to be a reaction formation, an unconscious defense against inadmissible hostility. Fanny is so afraid of disapproval that she either hides herself from others or makes her behavior conform to their expectations. She is so eager to accept the Grants' dinner invitation that she is afraid "she might not be able to appear properly submissive and indifferent" (II, v). It is a great relief when Sir Thomas says,

" 'She appears to feel as she ought.' " This is Fanny's project: to appear to feel as she ought. Spontaneity is out of the question. Both her feelings and her behavior are almost constantly determined by strategic necessities. She is so frightened, so anxious, so defensive, that she can hardly be aware of, much less express, her own thoughts and desires. She is freest with William, but even with him it is hard to imagine her expressing any but socially approved feelings.

Schachtel distinguishes two forms of the fixation in embeddedness, both of which we find in Fanny. One form "is the attempt to remain in or return to familial embeddedness, mainly embeddedness in the protection and parental love and care of a mothering person or of a mother or father substitute" *(M,* p. 75). The other form is the attempt to find safety "by completely accepting the closed pattern of . . . the world institutionalized in the particular culture . . . into which the individual is born and in which he is living." Fanny needs protection and parental love so desperately because she has never gotten them from her mother and father. Her substitutes are William, Edmund, and eventually Sir Thomas. She is in such dread of Sir Thomas early in the novel because he possesses absolute power and is the source of all true safety; if he rejects her, she is lost. She gains his protection and esteem by being true to his values even when he is absent, by completely accepting the world institutionalized in the subculture of Mansfield Park. Her greatest danger is in being misunderstood. She gets her reward when everyone sees how good and right she has been all along. We begin to understand why *Mansfield Park* strikes us as being so narrow and oppressive. It is a celebration of embeddedness and sterility.

The embedded person is afraid of life. He cannot cope. Because of his early traumatic or frustrating experiences, stimuli are threatening to him; he wants to escape into a womblike refuge. Fanny likes the solemnity of a peaceful night, the gravity of Mansfield after Sir Thomas returns, the serenity of her long empty hours with Aunt Bertram: "her perfect security in such a *tête-a-tête* from any sound of unkindness, was unspeakably welcome to a mind which had seldom known a pause in its alarms or embarrassments" (I, iv). Any change is hard on

Fanny. She is hysterical during her first week at Mansfield, and she goes into a decline after a few weeks in the hurly-burly of Portsmouth. Edmund explains to Mary that Fanny is "of all human creatures the one, over whom habit [has] most power, and novelty least . . . that [she can] tolerate nothing that [she is] not used to" (III, iv). The embedded person craves stability, peace, and order. Fanny clings to familiar people and to "the peace and tranquillity of Mansfield" (III, viii).

The severely embedded person relates to life in an infantile manner. He depends on the strength and benevolence of others with power, authority, or more strongly developed egos. He does not do, he suffers; and by his suffering he gets others to take responsibility for his well-being. As many critics have noted, Fanny is an almost totally passive heroine. She matures physically, but she remains psychologically a very young child. *Mansfield Park* is a wish fulfillment fantasy of embeddedness. The heroine does not grow up, but tries to cope with a frightening, rejecting world by being good, helpless, and unthreatening. As if by magic, her goodness is recognized, frightening people turn benign, persecutors and competitors are gotten rid of; she is married by the prince, adopted by the noble family, and lives happily ever after in the peace and tranquillity of the womblike world of Mansfield Park.

5

According to Karen Horney, neurosis begins as a defense against basic anxiety, which is a "profound insecurity and vague apprehensiveness" *(NHG,* p. 18) generated by feelings of isolation, helplessness, fear, and hostility. It involves a dread of the environment as a whole, which is "felt to be unreliable, mendacious, unappreciative, unfair, . . . begrudging . . . merciless."[10] As a result of this dread, the child develops self-protective strategies which in time become compulsive: "He cannot simply like or dislike, trust or distrust, express his wishes or protest against those of others, but has automatically to devise ways to cope with people and to manipulate them with minimum damage to himself."[11] He abandons himself in order to protect himself; but as the real self becomes weaker, the environment becomes more threatening.

Basic anxiety involves a fear not only of the environment, but also of the self. A threatening environment is bound to produce in the child both an intense hostility and a profound dependency which makes him terrified of expressing his hostility and compels him to repress it. Because he "registers within himself the existence of a highly explosive affect," he is fearful of himself, afraid that he will let out his rage and thus bring the world crashing down on his head.[12] The repression of hostility has severe consequences. It reinforces the child's feeling of defenselessness; it leads him to blame himself for the situation which makes him angry, to "feel unworthy of love" (NP, p. 84), and to fear spontaneity.

Basic anxiety affects the individual's attitudes toward both himself and others. He feels himself to be impotent, unlovable, of little value to the world. Because of his sense of weakness he wants to rely on others, to be protected and cared for; but he cannot risk himself with others because of his hostility and deep distrust. The invariable consequence of his basic anxiety "is that he has to put the greatest part of his energies into securing reassurance" (NP, p. 96). He seeks reassurance in his relation to others by developing the interpersonal strategies of defense which we shall examine next, and he seeks to compensate for his feelings of worthlessness and inadequacy by an intrapsychic process of self-glorification. These strategies constitute his effort to fulfill his highly intensified needs for safety, love and belonging, and self-esteem. They are also designed to reduce his anxiety and to provide a safe outlet for his hostility.

There are three main ways in which the child, and later the adult, can move in his effort to overcome his feelings of helplessness and isolation and to establish himself safely in a threatening world. He can adopt the self-effacing or compliant solution and move toward people; he can develop the aggressive or expansive solution and move against people; or he can become detached or resigned and move away from people. In each of the defensive moves one of the elements involved in basic anxiety is overemphasized: helplessness in the compliant solution, hostility in the aggressive solution, and isolation in the detached solution. Since under the conditions which produce anxiety all of these feelings are bound to arise, the individual will come to make all three of the defensive moves compulsively. They involve incompatible value systems and character structures, however; and a person cannot move in all of these directions without feeling confused and divided. Thus, order to gain some sense of wholeness and an ability to function, he will emphasize one move more than the others and will become predominantly compliant, aggressive, or detached. The other trends will continue to exist quite powerfully, but they will operate unconsciously and will manifest themselves in devious and disguised ways. Under the impetus of some powerful influence or of the dramatic failure of his predominant solution, the individual may embrace one of the repressed attitudes. He will experience this as conversion or education, but it will be merely the substitution of one defensive strategy for another.

The person in whom compliant trends are dominant tries to overcome his basic anxiety by gaining affection and approval and by controlling others through his need of them. He needs "to be liked, wanted, desired, loved; to feel accepted, welcomed, approved of, appreciated; to be needed, to be of importance to others, especially to one particular person; to be helped, protected, taken care of, guided" *(OIC,* p. 51). He needs to feel himself part of something larger and more powerful than himself, a need which often manifests itself as religious devotion, identification with a group or cause, or morbid dependency in a love relationship. His "self-esteem rises and falls" with the approval or disapproval of others, with "their affection or lack of it" *(OIC,* p. 54).

In order to gain the love, approval, acceptance, and support which he needs, the basically compliant person develops certain qualities, inhibitions, and ways of relating. He seeks to attach others to him by being good, loving, self-effacing, and weak. He tries to live up to the expectations of others, "often to the extent of losing sight of his own feelings" *(OIC,* p. 51). He becomes " 'unselfish,' self-sacrificing, undemanding . . . over-considerate, . . . over-appreciative, over-grateful, generous" *(OIC,* pp. 51-52). He is appeasing and conciliatory and tends to blame himself and to feel guilty whenever he quarrels with another, feels disappointed, or is criticized. Regarding himself as worthless or guilty makes him feel more secure, for then others cannot regard him as a threat. For similar reasons, "he tends to subordinate himself, takes second place, leaving the limelight to others" *(OIC,* p. 52). Because "any wish, any striving, any reaching out for more feels to him like a dangerous or reckless challenging of fate," he is severely inhibited in his self-assertive and self-protective activities and has powerful taboos against "all that is presumptuous, selfish, and aggressive" *(NHG,* pp. 218, 219).

The compliant defense brings with it not only certain ways of feeling and behaving, but also a special set of values. "They lie in the direction of goodness, sympathy, love, generosity, unselfishness, humility; while egotism, ambition, callousness, unscrupulousness, wielding of power are abhorred—though these attributes may at the same time be secretly admired because they represent 'strength' " *(OIC,* pp. 54-55). The compliant person does not hold his values as genuine ideals but because they are necessary to his defense system. He must believe in turning the other cheek, and he must see the world as displaying a providential order in which virtue is rewarded.

In the compliant person, says Horney, there are "a variety of aggressive tendencies strongly repressed" *(OIC,* p. 55). They are repressed because feeling them or acting them out would clash violently with the compliant person's need to feel that he is loving and unselfish and would radically endanger his whole strategy for gaining love and approval. His inner rage threatens his self-image, his philosphy of life, and his safety; and he must repress, disguise, or justify his anger in order to avoid arousing self-hate and the hostility of others.

The person in whom aggressive tendencies are predominant has goals, traits, and values which are quite the opposite of those of the compliant person. Since he seeks safety through conquest, "he needs to excel, to achieve success, prestige, or recognition" *(OIC,* p. 65). What appeals to him most is not love, but mastery. He abhors helplessness and is ashamed of suffering. He seeks to cultivate in himself "the efficiency and resourcefulness" necessary to his solution *(OIC,* p. 167).

There are three aggressive types: the narcissistic, the perfectionistic, and the arrogant-vindictive. They all "aim at mastering life. This is their way of conquering fears and anxieties: this gives meaning to their lives and gives them a certain zest for living" *(NHG,* p. 212). The narcissistic person seeks to master life "by self-admiration and the exercise of charm" *(NHG,* p. 212). He has an "unquestioned belief in his greatness and uniqueness," which gives him a "buoyancy and perennial youthfulness" *(NHG,* p. 194). The perfectionistic person "feels superior because of his high standards, moral and intellectual, and on this basis looks down on others" *(NHG,* p. 196). He may insist that others live up to "his standards of perfection and despise them for failing to do so" *(NHG,* p. 196). Through the height of his standards he compels fate. The arrogant-vindictive person is motivated chiefly by a need for vindictive triumphs. He is extremely competitive and must show his superiority to all rivals. He seeks to "exploit others, to outsmart them, to make them of use to himself" *(OIC,* p. 167). He avoids emotional involvement and dependency and uses the relations of friendship and marriage as a means by which he can possess the desirable qualities of others and so enhance his own position.

The basically detached person worships freedom and strives to be independent of both outer and inner demands. He pursues neither love nor mastery; he wants, rather, to be left alone, to have nothing expected of him and to be subject to no restrictions. He handles a threatening world by removing himself from its power and by shutting others out of his inner life. He disdains the pursuit of worldly success and has a profound aversion to effort. He makes himself invulnerable by being self-sufficient. This involves not only living in imagination, but also restricting his desires. In order to avoid being dependent on the environment, he tries to subdue his inner cravings and to be content with little. His resignation from active living makes him an onlooker toward both himself and others and often permits him to be an excellent observer of his own inner processes.

While the individual's interpersonal difficulties are creating movements toward, against, and away from people and the conflicts between them, his concomitant intrapsychic problems

43

are producing their own defensive strategies. The destructive attitudes of others, his alienation from his real self, and his own self-hatred make the individual feel weak and worthless. To compensate for this he creates, with the aid of his imagination, an "idealized image" of himself: "In this process he endows himself with unlimited powers and with exalted faculties; he becomes a hero, a genius, a supreme lover, a saint, a god" *(NHG,* p. 22). Thus begins his "search for glory," as "the energies driving toward self-realization are shifted to the aim of actualizing the idealized self" *(NHG,* p. 24).

The creation of the idealized image produces not only the search for glory but a whole structure of defensive strategies which Horney calls "the pride system." Self-idealization leads the individual to make both exaggerated *claims for* himself and excessive *demands upon* himself. He takes an intense pride in the attributes of his idealized self, and on the basis of these attributes he makes unrealistic claims upon others. He feels outraged unless he is treated in a way appropriate to his status as a special being. His claims make him extremely vulnerable, of course; for their frustration threatens to confront him with his "despised self," with the sense of worthlessness from which he is fleeing.

The individual's pride in his idealized self also leads him to impose stringent demands and taboos upon himself which Horney describes as "the tyranny of the should." The function of the shoulds is " to make oneself over into one's idealized self" *(NHG,* p. 68). Since the idealized image is for the most part a glorification of the self-effacing, expansive, or resigned solutions, the individual's shoulds are determined largely by the character traits and values associated with his predominant tendency. The shoulds are a defense against self-loathing, but they tend to aggravate the condition they are meant to cure. Not only do they increase self-alienation, but they also intensify self-hate, for they are impossible to live up to. The penalty for failure is the most severe feeling of worthlessness and self-contempt. This is why the shoulds have such tyrannical power.

6

When Fanny arrives at Mansfield Park at the age of ten, she has been already crushed by her experiences at home. She feels herself to be weak, worthless, inconsequential, and inadequate; and she is in the grip of a basic anxiety. Her defense system is already formed, and she displays many of the self-effacing traits which characterize her throughout the novel. She is "exceedingly timid and shy, and shrinking from notice" (I, ii). She is "ashamed of herself." She finds "something to fear in every person and place," creeps "about in constant terror of something or other," and often "retreat[s] toward her own chamber to cry." She is completely abject until she gains the friendship of Edmund. Fortified by his support, she begins to make a place for herself in the family by being useful and compliant: "if there were some amongst them whom she could not cease to fear, she began at least to know their ways, and to catch the best manner of conforming to them." She is "of an obliging, yielding temper," shows "a tractable disposition," and is pronounced, even by the supercilious Miss Bertrams, to be "good-natured enough." Edmund sees that she has "an affectionate heart, and a strong desire of doing right."

Fanny's insecurities are exacerbated by the treatment she receives at Mansfield Park. Almost everything conspires to make her feel like a nothing. She is criticized frequently, is constantly put in her place, and is made to feel like a person with no rights, no gifts, and no claims to consideration. She feels totally dependent and strives desperately to do whatever will gain her acceptance and enhance her security. She has little confidence in her capacities, perceptions, and judgments and in her ability to gain approval or to cope with new situations. She has no power to resist the negative image of herself which she receives from Mrs. Norris's continual deprecations, from the disdain of her girl cousins, and from the disapproval of Sir Thomas. She does not feel like a real person with a real place in the world. This is made evident when, late in the novel, she becomes a subscriber to a circulating library: she is "amazed at being any thing *in propria persona,* amazed at her own doings in every way; to be a renter, a chuser of books!" (III, ix).

Fanny's chief persecutor, as we have seen, is her Aunt Norris. She is terrified of Mrs. Norris, who is at first an important figure of authority; and in order to avoid her reproaches and the danger of her displeasure, she tries to think, feel, and behave exactly as her aunt prescribes. This is not difficult, for Mrs. Norris's injunctions correspond to the shoulds and taboos of Fanny's defense system. Mrs. Norris talks "to her the whole way from Northampton of her wonderful good fortune, and the extra-ordinary degree of gratitude and good behavior which it ought to produce" (I, ii); and Fanny does her utmost to be grateful and well behaved. Since this seems to be the condition of her acceptance at Mansfield Park, she is in dread of being thought ungrateful or naughty; and she experiences great anxiety at the least hint of disapproval. She constantly hears that she will be "a very obstinate, ungrateful girl, if she does not do what her aunt and cousins wish her" (I, xv); and whenever she can do so without violating principles, she slavishly complies with their demands. Aunt Norris says that she should always be "lowest and last," and Fanny anxiously shuns any form of notice or distinction. She accepts the various deprivations imposed by her aunt as "perfectly reasonable. She rated her own claims to comfort as low as even Mrs. Norris could" (II, v).

Fanny is not secure enough even to resent the way in which she is abused. She is "often mortified" by her cousins' treatment of her, but she thinks "too lowly of her own claims to feel injured by it" (I, ii). She thinks so lowly of her own claims partly because of her damaged self-esteem and her taboos against presumption and partly because she is afraid to feel injured. To be angry with others for their treatment of her is to risk their anger in return and possibly their rejection. This she cannot do. She must handle abuse by belittling herself, by feeling that the way she is treated is perfectly reasonable, considering her inconsequence. Any recognition, any triumph, threatens to upset this solution; and Fanny responds by anxiously reaffirming her unworthiness. Her taboos against pride are so powerful that she does not even take satisfaction in her own humility—though the author makes sure that it is properly appreciated.

Fanny's defenses are, broadly speaking, of two kinds: those designed to prevent dangerous situations from arising and those designed to secure reassurance and protection. The preventive defenses include self-minimization; self-accusation; avoidance of attention, competition, and triumph; and taboos against pride, envy, and resentment. Fanny does not want to do anything which will arouse antagonism, expose her to judgment, or jeopardize her acceptance. She feels safest when others cannot possibly regard her as a threat. The less attention she attracts and the less recognition she receives, the less likely she is to be an object of criticism or envy. As Mary Crawford observes, Fanny is "almost as fearful of notice and praise as other women [are] of neglect" (II, iii). Fanny is acutely self-conscious. Being the focus of attention when she enters a room, speaks, or dances is an ordeal for her.

Most of Fanny's preventive defenses are generated by her self-effacing trends; but this set of defenses includes also her strong tendencies toward withdrawal, resignation, and detachment. She frequently hides away in the East room, which is her "nest of comforts" (I, xvi), her retreat, her refuge from the buffets and alarms of daily life. She is "not often invited to join in the conversation of others, nor [does] she desire it. Her own thoughts and reflections [are] habitually her best companions" (I, viii). She turns for her pleasures to such solitary occupations as reading or to the contemplation of nature; she does not expect to get much from other human beings. To avoid being judged, she keeps her thoughts and feelings to herself. She is "always so gentle and retiring" that Sir Thomas finds "her emotions" to be "beyond his discrimination" (III, v). Since having wishes seems dangerous, Fanny tries hard to accept what is given and to want nothing for herself. She is easily satisfied and does not complain, even to herself, about her deprivations. She does what she is told, but she never initiates activity. If she is passive and subservient, there is less danger that she will step out of her place or do something wrong. Her most common roles are those of servant and spectator. Her onlooker attitude, combined with her defensive alertness, makes her a good observer of others; she sees more than people who are active and involved.

Fanny seeks reassurance and protection in three major ways: by being useful, by being good, and by attaching herself to a stronger and more favored member of the family, someone who can watch out for her needs and intercede on her behalf with the powerful parental figure.

Fanny needs to be useful, needs to be needed, in order to compensate for her feelings of worthlessness and inconsequentiality. " 'I can never,' " she tells Edmund, " 'be important to any one' " (I, iii). She arrives at Mansfield Park with this feeling. At home she had served as "play-fellow, instructress, and nurse" to her younger brothers and sisters (I, ii); but she was neglected by both her mother and father and was felt, as a "delicate and puny" child (I, i) in a large family, to be something of a nuisance, at best superfluous. When she leaves, no one, with the exception of William, misses her. She is delighted, therefore, to be of use to her aunts, to her cousins, to the actors in the play, to anyone who will make her feel that her existence is of some importance. She would be reconciled even to living with Aunt Norris if her aunt really wanted her: " 'it would be delightful to feel myself of consequence to any body!' " (I, iii). Since she has no inner feeling of worth, Fanny depends upon others to give value to her life and becomes depressed and anxious when she cannot be of service. She becomes so deeply attached to her Aunt Bertram partly because her aunt is so dependent upon her for comfort. Her aunt's repeated assertions that she cannot do without Fanny are sweet music to her ears. When she returns to Portsmouth, she dreams "of being of consequence" to her mother (III, viii) as she had never been before. With the disappointment of these hopes, she begins to long for Mansfield and to think of it as her true home: "Could she have been at home, she might have been of service to every creature in the house. She felt that she must have been of use to all. To all, she must have saved some trouble of head or hand" (III, xiv). When disasters fall upon the Bertrams and everyone turns to her for comfort, Fanny is happy.

Fanny is profoundly insecure not only about her worth, her consequence, but also about her status. She is acutely aware of her marginal position at Mansfield Park and feels that she can be expelled at any time, returned to a home where no one wants her, should she fail to give satisfaction. She derives from Mrs. Norris the impression that she can assure her continued acceptance only by being very, very good. She is in dread of Sir Thomas, as we have seen, because he is a stern man who wields an absolute power over her fate. Her security depends upon his approval, his belief in her goodness. Being good involves, essentially, being grateful and obedient and conforming to the principles of morality and decorum taught by Edmund and enforced by Sir Thomas. Aunt Norris is such a terrible enemy because she is constantly denying Fanny's goodness, accusing her of self-will and ingratitude; and Fanny is afraid that Sir Thomas will accept her judgments. Edmund, on the other hand, knows that she really is good and provides a precious reassurance. Fanny proves her goodness by behaving exactly as Sir Thomas would have wished during his absence. She is overwhelmed by anxiety when her refusal to accept Henry Crawford arouses her uncle's ire: "The past, present, future, every thing was terrible . . . Selfish and ungrateful! to have appeared so to him! She was miserable for ever" (III, i). Her uncle's provision of a fire, even in these circumstances, calms her greatly; it means that she is a part of the family, with recognized rights, even though she has given displeasure. In the end, of course, her goodness is more than vindicated; she is celebrated as little less than angelic.

It is difficult to feel as positively about Fanny's goodness as Jane Austen wishes us to. Hers is the goodness of a terrified child who dreads total rejection if she does not conform in every way to the will of those in power. It is rigid, desperate, compulsive. Fanny is not actively loving or benevolent; she is obedient, submissive, driven by her fears and her shoulds. Her goodness provides, moreover, the only outlet for her repressed aggressive impulses. She stands up to others, occasionally, in the name of her principles. She is highly critical of many of the people around her, either inwardly or with Edmund; but she gets around her taboos against aggression and presumption by attacking on the side of authority and in the name of virtue. She is, in truth, a prig.

Given her timidity, her dependency, her inability to assert herself in the face of neglect, abuse, and injustice, Fanny would be lost without a protector. Despite their differences in personality, William and Edmund play this role for her in remarkably similar ways. William is "her constant companion and friend; her advocate with her mother (of whom he was the darling) in every distress" (I, ii). At Mansfield Park, she is in a state of panic until Edmund befriends her, helps her write to her brother, and recognizes her goodness: "From this day Fanny grew more comfortable." As his behavior at cards makes clear (II, vii), William has an aggressive personality. Fanny subordinates herself to him; and he, in turn, looks out for her interests and intercedes with their mother on her behalf. Edmund is compliant. He makes up for his inferior position as second son by being good; and, as a result, he becomes the favorite of his father. He identifies with Fanny as a kindred spirit and takes an immense moral pleasure in being good to her. Like William, he is sensitive to Fanny's weakness and hovers about her with a kind of parental solicitude, forcing others to be considerate. He is not himself a dominating personality (like William); but his influence in the household, especially with his father, makes him a source of security; and Fanny sees him as her hero, her champion. She becomes quite worried when Sir Thomas looks reproachfully at Edmund on learning of his participation in the play (II, i). Eventually, of course, Sir Thomas himself becomes Fanny's protector, and then she is completely safe.

7

Now that Fanny's character structure and defensive strategies have been analyzed, it is possible to understand her relationships with other characters and her behavior in various episodes. Jane Austen's characterization is so rich that it is almost inexhaustible. I shall concentrate upon some major aspects of Fanny's behavior in the play episode, her relationship with Henry Crawford, her visit to Portsmouth, and her triumphant return home.

No detailed reasons are given for Fanny's opposition to the play. Until Edmund decides to act, her sentiments, presumably, are the same as his. The central issue for Fanny is respect for the authority of Sir Thomas: " 'he would never,' " says Edmund, " 'wish his grown up daughters to be acting plays. His sense of decorum is strict' " (I, xiii). When *Lovers' Vows* is chosen, the offense is compounded. Fanny is astonished that so "improper" a play "could be proposed and accepted in a private Theatre," and she longs to have her cousins "roused as soon as possible by the remonstrance which Edmund would certainly make" (I, xv). Even Lady Bertram urges them not to " 'act anything improper . . . Sir Thomas would not like it.' " As we have seen, Fanny is in dread of Sir Thomas. The idea of challenging, usurping, or disobeying his authority is extremely frightening to her. Fanny protects herself in this threatening situation by identifying with Sir Thomas as he is represented by Edmund, the good son; by refusing to participate; and by making clear, to herself at least, how much she disapproves of what is going on. Her censoriousness reassures her that *she* is a good girl and that she will not, therefore, be an object of Sir Thomas's wrath. She is deeply disturbed when Edmund decides to act. She is torn between her impulse to submit to him and her need to disapprove; she is distressed at this sign of Mary Crawford's power; and she is afraid of the danger in which his complicity will place her protector. When Sir Thomas returns home, her "solicitude on Edmund's account [is] indescribable" (II, i).

Fanny's refusal to act is only partially motivated by her fear of Sir Thomas. Her initial reaction is prompted chiefly by her dread of exposing herself:

> "You must be Cottager's wife."
>
> "Me!" cried Fanny, sitting down again with a most frightened look. "Indeed you must excuse me. I could not act any thing if you were to give me the world. No, indeed, I cannot act."
>
> ". . . It is not that I am afraid of learning by heart," said Fanny, shocked to find herself at that moment the only speaker in the room, and to feel that almost every eye was upon her; "but I really cannot act." (I, xv)

Fanny is not saying that she will not act or feels that she should not act, but that she cannot act: " 'It would be absolutely impossible for me.' " Her reaction is quite understandable in the light of her need for obscurity, her acute self-consciousness, her fear of attention. If she is "shocked" to find herself the only speaker in the room, she would be traumatized by having to appear on a stage, an object of scrutiny and judgment.

Despite her evident panic, Fanny's refusal is not accepted. Tom persists in his request and is urgently backed by Maria, Mr. Crawford, and Mr. Yates. Fanny is quite overpowered; and before she can catch her breath, Mrs. Norris joins in with the charge that she will be " 'a very obstinate, ungrateful girl, if she does not do what her aunt and counsins wish her.' " Edmund and Mary Crawford give Fanny what moral support they can, but she is badly shaken by this experience.

We must see Fanny as a person if we are to feel the dramatic intensity of this situation and to understand the extent of her confusion and distress. She fears a repetition of the assault, with "Edmund perhaps away" (I, xvi). Can she stand up to "all the authoritative urgency that Tom and Maria [are] capable of?" She is not sure, moreover, what she *ought* to do. Mrs. Norris struck a nerve when she accused Fanny of ingratitude. Fanny is caught in a conflict between several of her self-effacing shoulds. She must not do what Sir Thomas would disapprove of, but she must not be selfish or ungrateful either: "Was she *right* in refusing what was so . . . strongly wished for? What might be so essential to a scheme on which some of those to whom she owed the greatest complaisance, had set their hearts? Was it not ill-nature—selfishness—and a fear of exposing herself? . . . It would be so horrible to her to act, that she was inclined to suspect the truth and purity of her own scruples." It is of the utmost importance to Fanny to do what is right, but she cannot "find her way to duty," and she is emotionally paralyzed. She hopes that Edmund will at once relieve her moral anxiety and save her from having to perform by assuring her that to act would be wrong, but he has decided that he must take a part himself in order to confine the evil.

When Fanny is asked again, Edmund answers for her, and she is saved. But she has not resolved her conflict. When she is asked to aid in rehearsal by reading a part, she cannot refuse: "As they all persevered—as Edmund repeated his wish, and with a look of even fond dependence on her good nature, she must yield . . . . Everybody was satisfied—and she [was] left to the tremors of a most palpitating heart" (I, xviii). At this critical juncture Fanny is saved from a possible nervous collapse and from a possible charge of complicity by the arrival of Sir Thomas. We never learn if reading would have been wrong.

Fanny does, in fact, become quite involved in the production of the play, but in ways which do not arouse her various anxieties. Once she has been saved from having to act, she finds herself quite left out; and this arouses her old feelings of inconsequence. Everyone else is "gay and busy, prosperous and important." "She alone was sad and insignificant; she had no share in any thing; she might go or stay . . . without being seen or missed. She could almost think any thing would have been preferable to this" (I, xvii). She compensates for her feeling of insignificance in the usual way, by serving: "The gloom of her first anticipations was proved to have been unfounded. She was occasionally useful to all; she was perhaps as much at peace as any. There was a great deal of needlework to be done, moreover, in which her help was wanted." (I, xviii). Fanny's behavior in the play episode is consistent throughout with our understanding of her character; but from a thematic point of view, it is difficult to understand the difference between acting and sewing.

It is during a discussion of the play while they are dining at the Grants' that Henry Crawford first becomes attracted to Fanny. When Henry expresses a wish that Sir Thomas's return had been delayed, Fanny replies:

> "As far as *I* am concerned, sir, I would not have delayed his return for a day. My uncle disapproved it all so entirely when he did arrive, that in my opinion, everything had gone quite far enough."
> She had never spoken so much at once to him in her life before, and never so angrily to any one; and when her speech was over, she trembled and blushed at her own daring. He was surprised; but after a few moments silent consideration of her, replied in a calmer, graver tone, and as if the candid result of conviction, "I believe you are right. It

was more pleasant than prudent. . . . " And then turning the conversation, he would have engaged her on some other subject, but her answers were so shy and reluctant that he could not advance in any way. (II, v)

Henry is an expansive person who prides himself on his charm and his ability to capture the hearts of women. He is accustomed to being pursued or to making easy conquests. He is attracted to Fanny in part because she presents an unusual challenge which, for the sake of his pride, he is determined to meet:

> "I was never so long in company with a girl in my life—trying to entertain her—and succeed so ill! Never met with a girl who looked so grave on me! I must try to get the better of this. Her looks say, 'I will not like you, I am determined not to like you,' and I say, she shall." (II, vi)

Henry is attracted also by Fanny's moral rectitude. There is a side of him which is self-condemning and which leads him to accept Fanny's rebuke. He sees Fanny as a moral superior and hopes to be more at peace with himself by submitting to her values and gaining her approval. In effect, Fanny has hurt his pride and activated his conscience; both his expansive and his self-effacing shoulds require him to win her love and approval.

Henry's initial plan is to remain heart-whole himself, but to make Fanny feel, when he goes away, " 'that she shall never be happy again.' " In this way he will restore his pride and will get revenge on her for having made him doubt his powers. As he comes to know Fanny, however, he is genuinely attracted; and he determines to win her hand in marriage. He decides to marry her in part, I suspect, because he is having no success in flirting; an offer of marriage, he feels, will be irresistible. But he also wishes to possess for himself certain qualities which he sees Fanny display toward others and which he feels will be his once he wins her heart. He imagines her being as affectionate as she is toward William, as cheerfully subservient as she is toward her aunts, and as grateful as she is toward anyone who does her the smallest kindness. Her "dependent, helpless . . . neglected" (II, xii) state feeds his sense of power; he will transform her life. What a reward will he not deserve from her! Marrying such a deprived creature and doing so much for her will make him feel virtuous. Her principles will give him every assurance of her fidelity and will help him to avoid moral uneasiness and self-disgust. Her continued resistance even after his proposal makes "her affection appear of greater consequence, because it was withheld, and determine[s] him to have the *glory,* as well as the felicity, of forcing her to love him" (III, ii; my italics). He "derives[s] spirits" from the "difficulty."

Henry's glorification of Fanny is a bit overstrained, making one suspect authorial manipulation; but, on the whole, his behavior toward her is in keeping with his character. Given *her* character, Fanny could never love a man like Henry Crawford, despite Jane Austen's assurances that Henry would have had a chance if Fanny's heart had not been already engaged or if Edmund had married Mary. The author wishes us to believe in Henry's chances for thematic purposes, so we will feel that he has destroyed himself, that he could have been rewarded had he remained virtuous.

Fanny has a serious objection, of course, to Henry's moral character. She has observed his flirtations with Maria and Julia, and she has " 'received an impression which will never be got over' " (III, iv). When, at the Grants, Henry remarks that he was "never happier" than during the period of the play, Fanny is full of "silent indignation": " 'never happier than when behaving so dishonourably and unfeelingly!—Oh! what a corrupted mind!' " (II, v). When Henry begins his attentions, Fanny surmises, quite correctly, that "he wanted . . . to cheat her of her tranquillity as he had cheated" her cousins of theirs (II, viii). He eventually overcomes her distrust of his affection, but he never convinces her of his virtue. He makes some progress in this direction at Portsmouth, but Fanny is not much disillusioned when he runs off with Maria. Given her need to be good, to be allied with someone who shares her values, and to be protected by someone whom she trusts completely, Fanny could never bring herself to marry a man as tainted in her mind as Henry Crawford.

Henry tries to assure Fanny of his virtue by praising hers: " 'You are infinitely my superior in merit; all *that* I know' " (III, iii). But this is exactly what Fanny does not like to hear. She does not like to be admired, to be praised, to be placed in a position of leadership and superiority. When Henry says that her judgment is his " 'rule of right,' " Fanny replies, " 'Oh, no!—do not say so' " (III, xi). She reacts similarly to Edmund's assertion that her guidance will remedy Crawford's defects of character, that she " 'will make him everything' ": " 'I would not engage in such a charge,' " cried Fanny in a shrinking accent—" 'in such an office of high responsibility!' " (III, iv). Insofar as Henry's attentions feed her pride and bring triumph and glory, they are frightening to Fanny. Mary Crawford hopes to recommend her brother's suit by reminding Fanny of the "envy" of other women and " 'the glory of fixing one who has been shot at by so many' " (III, v). These things would be gratifying to the expansive Mary, but they are repugnant to the self-effacing Fanny.

Fanny is quite right when she tells Edmund that " 'there were never two people more dissimilar,' " that it is " 'quite impossible' " that she and Henry Crawford could " 'ever be tolerably happy together, even if [she] *could* like him' " (III, iv). Henry Crawford is a brilliant, restless, gregarious man; Fanny is the opposite. She would be overwhelmed as Henry's wife, and he would soon come to be dissatisfied with her social limitations. Fanny senses this. The prospect of such a marriage is repellent to her. Even if Edmund were out of the picture, Fanny could never marry a man like Henry Crawford. She would rather be a spinster and remain safe at Mansfield.

As long as Edmund is in the picture, Fanny must love him. Understanding why Henry Crawford is so unsuitable helps us to see the appeal of Edmund. Fanny feels him to be her mentor, her moral superior, her friend, champion, and protector. She trusts his good will completely. He is the only person, other than her brother William, to whom she can speak with any degree of openness. They are entirely compatible in tastes, inclinations, and life styles; they are "equally formed for domestic life, and attached to country pleasures" (III, xvii). They will share a life of serenity, repose, and mutual approbation. Their happiness may not be sublime, but it will be "secure." With Edmund there will be no challenges which Fanny cannot meet.

When Fanny sees that Henry Crawford seriously wants to marry her, that he seeks her for "her gentleness, and her goodness" (III, ii), and that he has secured William's promotion for her sake, she has "a sensation of being honored" and a feeling of "gratitude"; but for the most part she is oppressed by the situation into which his attentions have placed her. Henry threatens her security by bringing down upon her Sir Thomas's wrath. Sir Thomas is angry mainly because he does not understand the grounds of Fanny's refusal. She does not tell him of her objections to Crawford because this would implicate her cousins; and she has a strong taboo against being critical of others, especially of those toward whom she must repress her envy and resentment. Nor can she tell him that she loves another because this would arouse his suspicions about Edmund. She must keep her love a secret in order to avoid family resentment and the charge of presumption. When Edmund falls in love with Mary, Fanny struggles to feel as she ought: "To call or to fancy it a loss, a disappointment, would be a presumption; for which she had not words enough to satisfy her own humility" (II, ix). She is in a painful position with Edmund also. He is constantly promoting her marriage with Crawford and confiding his love for her detested rival. It is no wonder that when, in Portsmouth, Fanny begins to think better of Crawford, her highest hope is that "he would not much longer persevere in a suit so distressing to her" (III, xi). This is the only way, it seems, in which she can be freed of Edmund's urgings and restored to Sir Thomas's favor.

The Portsmouth episode has attracted critical attention because of the obvious disparity between Jane Austen's approving view of Fanny, which is reflected in the chorus of praise that increasingly surrounds her, and Fanny's snobbish attitudes and unattractive behavior toward her family. She seems excessively cold and critical, embarrassed and ashamed. Instead of having sympathy for her overburdened mother, she is preoccupied with self-pity and her nostalgia for "the genteel and well-appointed" (III, xii). We shall find that here, as elsewhere, Fanny's behavior is more intelligible, and we are more sympathetic, when Fanny is seen as a person rather than as a heroine.

The prospect of returning home awakens Fanny's hunger for love and belonging. Both in her early years in Portsmouth and in her stay at Mansfield Park, she has been starved for parental affection, for love, warmth, and tender concern. Her father never showed her "anything approaching to tenderness" (III, viii). And her mother, "occupied by the incessant demands of a house full of little children" (III, vi), partial to the boys, and "alienated . . . by the helplessness and fretfulness of a fearful temper," was either hostile or indifferent to Fanny. At Mansfield Park, Sir Thomas is remote and stern, Mrs. Norris is an enemy, and Lady Bertram is a passive figure who does not give but requires indulgent care. Fanny has handled this deprivation by blaming herself, by resigning her claims, and by making do with parent substitutes, like William and Edmund. Feeling that she had probably "been unreasonable in wanting a larger share than any one among so many could deserve," and that she has therefore been sent away, she learns at Mansfield "how to be useful and how to forbear," so as to avoid a second rejection. Her need for love has not disappeared, however; and the thought of returning home awakens fantasies of gratification. She dreams of being "in the centre" of the family "circle," of being "loved by so many, and more loved by all than she had ever been before," of feeling "affection without fear or restraint," of feeling "herself the equal of those who surrounded her." She will "now find a warm and affectionate friend" in her mother; they will "soon be what mother and daughter ought to be to each other."

She is, of course, severely disappointed by the treatment she receives. Her father seems "inclined to forget her" (III, vii) shortly after her arrival; her mother still has "neither leisure nor affection to bestow on Fanny" (III, viii); and the other children, with the exception of William and Susan, are favored rivals to whom she is of little or no importance. She handles her resentment, at first, in a variety of defensive ways. She is being "unreasonable" (III, vii). She has no "right . . . to be of importance to her family." "William's concerns must be dearest"; perhaps in a few days, when the *Thrush* has sailed, there will be time and attention for her. But it does "pain her to have Mansfield forgotten; the friends who had done so much—the dear, dear friends!" The pain of neglect, which she is afraid to feel on her own behalf, she is free to feel on behalf of others.

Before the week is over it is "all disappointment"; her home is "the very reverse of what she could have wished" (III, viii). In the bitterness of her disillusionment, with nothing left to hope for, Fanny allows her resentment to show:

> She might scruple to make use of the words, but she must and did feel that her mother was a partial, ill-judging parent, a dawdle, a slattern, who neither taught nor restrained her children, whose house was the scene of mismanagement and discomfort from beginning to end, and who had no talent, no conversation, no affection toward herself; no curiosity to know her better, no desire of her friendship, and no inclination for her company that could lessen her sense of such feelings.

These are the harshest thoughts that Fanny has toward anyone in the whole course of the novel. They reflect not only her current disappointment, but also her resentment of earlier deprivation, memories of which now begin to surface. When Fanny returns to Portsmouth, she is in a vulnerable state; she is allowing herself to crave the love and acceptance which have always been denied to her. Her frustration is proportional to the intensity of her desire, and her hostility is proportional to her frustration. She is in no condition to see things from any perspective other than her own; she is bitterly hurt and angry.

Fanny does not express or act out her rage, of course; she is much too insecure for that. She reverts to her usual defenses of modesty, usefulness, and withdrawal. She devotes herself to the appreciative Susan. She continues, however, to be inwardly critical of her parents and their home. This is partly an expression of her anger and partly a defense against self-hate. She has violated her taboo against feeling resentment; and she must assure herself of her righteousness by tearing down her family, by convincing herself that they deserve her condemnation. She validates her judgments by identifying her criteria of propriety with those of Mansfield Park, which she now glorifies and invests with absolute moral authority. There, whatever is, is right. She is so embarrassed by her family because she is so critical of them. It is humiliating to be identified with a set of people and a life style which she has thoroughly condemned. She is acutely distressed when Henry Crawford arrives partly because she fears that he will associate her with her family and will heap upon her the contempt which she has been feeling toward them.

Fanny's feelings on return to Mansfield Park are as immature, and as understandable, as are her responses to Portsmouth; and, again, an analysis of them helps to explain why reader response and authorial rhetoric often part ways. Jane Austen has set herself a difficult artistic problem. Fanny's happiness comes at the expense of others, not only of her enemies, but of her friends as well. Through much of the denouement, Edmund, Sir Thomas, and Lady Bertram are quite miserable; but Fanny is happy, and we are supposed to rejoice. Austen speaks frequently of Fanny's sympathetic sufferings, which are no doubt genuine, and explains why she "must have been happy in spite of every thing" (III, xvii); but there is a euphoria about Fanny, and at times a kind of glee, which seem inappropriate to the gravity of the situation. When she first hears the news about Crawford and Maria, she thinks it "scarcely possible" for Sir Thomas and Edmund "to support life and reason under such a disgrace; and it appeared to her, that as far as this world was concerned, the greatest blessing to every one of kindred with Mrs. Rushworth would be instant annihilation" (III, xv). But as soon as she is summoned home, she is "exquisitely happy." She fights against such feelings, recognizing their selfishness and insensitivity; but she cannot suppress them. In the company of the dejected Edmund, "her heart swell[s] with joy and gratitude" as she leaves Portsmouth; and "her perceptions and her pleasures [are] of the keenest sort" as she enters the grounds of Mansfield Park.

Here, as in Portsmouth, Fanny is so immersed in her own sensations that she cannot be sensitive to the problems of others. Before she receives news of the Crawford-Maria affair, she is "very low" (III, xi). Portsmouth is hateful, her health is declining, and she feels "deserted by everybody" who is of importance to her. She cannot think of Henry's "returning to town, and being frequently with Mary and Edmund, without feelings so near akin to envy, as made her hate herself for having them." She longs for Mansfield Park, which she now recognizes as her only home; but she is powerless to return until she is sent for. The Crawfords offer to take her back; but "her awe of her uncle, and her dread of taking a liberty with him" (III, xiv) make it impossible for her to accept. Henry Crawford's attentions continue to threaten her relations with her uncle; as long as she must decline Henry without being able to explain herself, she is in danger of being thought rebellious and ungrateful. Although Mary's character looks worse and worse, there seems every likelihood that Edmund will marry her, and Fanny expects every day to hear the dreaded news. If Edmund marries Mary, she will be frustrated in love, cut off from her protector, and exposed all the more to Henry's pursuit.

It is no wonder that with the sudden change of events Fanny becomes euphorically happy. She has stepped out of a nightmare into a dream come true. One after another, the obstacles to her wishes are removed: "She was returned to Mansfield Park, she was useful, she was beloved; she was safe from Mr. Crawford, and when Sir Thomas came back she had every proof . . . of his perfect approbation and increased regard; . . . Edmund was no longer the dupe of Miss Crawford" (III, xvii). At this point, what is a nightmare for others brings about the realization of her most cherished fantasies. She cannot help having a sense of triumph, of exultation. When Edmund begins to love her, the hopes and dreams which she had felt it presumptuous to acknowledge even to herself are coming true. We may not wish Fanny's kind of happiness for ourselves, but for her it is perfect. No situation could be better adapted to her needs than to be the wife of Edmund, the beloved daughter of Sir Thomas, and the mistress of Mansfield parsonage.

8

Fanny Price is one of the great mimetic characters in English fiction. Jane Austen's intuitive grasp and concrete portrayal of her psychology are amazing. To some, her misinterpretation of Fanny, her glorification of strategic motives and unhealthy traits, may also seem remarkable. How could Austen have portrayed Fanny so well and judged her so ill?

Novelists are more gifted than the rest of us in many ways, but they are no less subject to psychological limitations. They, too, have blind spots when it comes to their own defensive strategies and their own destructive solutions, however perceptive they might be in analyzing and judging other and opposite types. They, too, need to justify their values and to believe that their solutions are well-adapted to the world. *Mansfield Park* is clearly a glorification of the self-effacing solution. Fanny is the exemplar of this solution; and the novel as a whole is a fantasy of her strategies working to perfection, much better than they usually do in life.

There is a certain amount of manipulation in the removal of blocking forces. Edmund's love for Fanny is neither depicted nor explained; it is simply a part of the fairy-tale atmosphere which dominates at the end. The manner in which the Crawfords are removed has caused considerable uneasiness among Austen's readers. Part of the explanation, I believe, is that the Crawfords are too fully rendered to be merely villains in the comic action but not rendered fully enough, particularly at the end, to be entirely believable as people. When antagonists are rendered as persons, as Henry and, to a lesser degree, Mary are, we tend to find them more interesting and sympathetic than we should, given their comic roles and their moral characters.

Jane Austen does not manipulate her main character in the least. She is a creation inside a creation and is mimetically rendered throughout. This, as I have suggested, creates an appetite for a thoroughgoing realism. The ending, however, strikes us not as true to experience, but as an indulgence of the heroine. It shows the triumph of the self-effacing protagonist over her aggressive enemies. The author presides, dispensing justice and making Fanny's dreams come true. Jane Austen is as harsh upon the aggressive characters as she is indulgent to the "good" ones. She has no blind spots here. She sees their faults, understands the damage which has been done by their upbringing, and calls attention to the self-destructiveness, and ultimate failure, of their solutions. One reason why we may have some sympathy for the Crawfords is that the author has loaded the dice against them. She has made them behave worse, or at least more stupidly, than we had expected they would. Mary may have wished for Tom's death, but she would never have revealed such sentiments to Fanny.

In order for *Mansfield Park* to have its desired effect, the reader must be sympathetic to the defense system of the implied author, with its accompanying values and fantasies. A reader who approaches it from a different perspective will find himself alienated by the heroine, at war with the author, and, in some cases, in league with the villains.

3

Emma

1

Emma is, like *Mansfield Park,*
a controversial novel. The chief issues are the genuineness of
Emma's reformation and the felicity of her marriage to Knightley. Most critics feel that Jane Austen means for us to see
Emma's self-knowledge as profound, her education as permanent, and her marriage as perfectly happy, and that the author's
interpretation is correct. There are two minority positions. One
is that Emma does not grow as much as Austen thinks she does
and that the ending is not as happy as the rhetoric makes it
seem. The other is that Austen is aware of the limitations of her
heroine's growth and happiness and that she does not really
mean for us to see Emma's character and situation at the end as
ideal.

This controversy becomes intelligible, I believe, when we
see that Emma is, like Fanny Price, a creation inside a creation.
She is the heroine of the comic action and the character whose

education constitutes the novel's thematic center, but she is also an imagined human being whose personal qualities are not always in harmony with her dramatic and thematic functions. Most critics are not troubled by a sense of conflict in the novel because they do not respond to Emma as though she were a person; they see her only as an aesthetic and an illustrative character. The critics who see the ending as open, or ironic, or subtly critical of the society into which Emma is absorbed do respond to her as a person. They then ascribe to the novel a thematic structure which fits their perceptions of her character. I am in agreement with those who feel that the novel's rhetoric is in conflict with its concrete portrayal of life. Both as a comedy and as a novel of education, *Emma* encourages a favorable view of the protagonist's happiness and growth. When Emma is understood psychologically, however, it is evident that her change is neither complete nor entirely for the better, and that her marriage to Knightley signifies not so much an entrance into maturity as a regression to childish dependency.

2

As a comic structure, *Emma* is composed of three love relationships with their corresponding blocking forces. The happiness of Emma and Knightley is threatened by Emma's faults and illusions, by the lovers' unconsciousness of their feelings for each other, and by Mr. Woodhouse's opposition to marriage. Jane Fairfax and Frank Churchill are blocked by Mrs. Churchill. Harriet Smith and Robert Martin are thwarted by the interference of Emma. Each of the protagonists undergoes a period of distress as his or her happiness seems about to be frustrated; the blocking forces are removed by a series of rapid reversals; and there is a flurry of weddings at the end. All obstacles to happiness are overcome. Mistakes are acknowledged, transgressions are forgiven, and conflicts between love and duty are resolved. The marriages are all socially suitable and based on love. No one, it turns out, has been permanently harmed.

"The humor in comedy," says Frye, "is usually someone with a good deal of social prestige and power, who is able to force much of the play's society into line with his obsession" *(AC,* p. 169). The most important humor in *Emma* is Emma herself, who fulfills the role both of romantic heroine and of the *alazon* or imposter who is the major blocking force. Emma's "humors" or obsessions are many, and they give rise to a variety of mistakes and illusions. She is an "imaginist," a snob, an arranger of other people's lives. She prides herself on her own elegance and "Understanding" and is obsessed with her superiority and importance. She imposes an irrational law of celibacy upon herself and insists upon an unsuitably grand marriage for Harriet Smith. "The social judgment against the absurd is closer to the comic norm," says Frye, "than the moral judgment against the wicked" *(AC,* p. 168). Emma becomes more and more absurd as she ritually repeats her obsessions. Her repentances, which she repeats with almost equal frequency, keep her from seeming wicked. She is opposed by Knightley, who plays the role of "the plain dealer, an outspoken advocate of a kind of moral norm who has the sympathy of the audience" *(AC,* p. 176). The comic resolution depends upon Emma's being purged of her humors and brought round to Knightley's point of view. When we respond to the novel as a comedy, we have no doubt that this happens; and, as Frye observes, "whatever emerges is supposed to be there for good" *(AC,* p. 170).

The new society which crystallizes at the end is not only more clear-sighted; it is also better ordered and morally more secure. The mystery of Harriet's birth is removed, and she enters her proper social sphere. The capricious Mrs. Churchill is dead, and the relationship between Frank and Jane can become open and honorable. Most important of all, Emma accepts subordination to a proper authority. She has had too much power and independence. Her marriage to Knightley brings back to Hartfield the moral order which had disappeared with the death of her mother.

The tone of *Emma* is notably different from that of *Mansfield Park.* Both novels have comic structures; but *Emma* is amusing and gay, whereas *Mansfield Park* is serious and somber. *Emma* is full of humors characters who are wittily portrayed and who repeat their obsessions with delightful regularity. It abounds in ironies and misunderstandings and gives us all the fun of a comedy of errors. *Mansfield Park* specializes in the creation and removal of anxiety. Its satisfactions are those which accompany the gradual lifting of a nightmare and its eventual transformation into a wish fulfillment fantasy. There is nothing amusing about Fanny's plight, and the blocking characters are far more ominous than funny. Emma is presented as essentially secure; and we are free to laugh at her difficulties, most of which she brings upon herself. It is only after the Box Hill episode that her discomfiture becomes truly painful. Her subsequent vision of a bleak future is the darkest moment in the book, but it is quickly followed not only by her deliverance but also by a general rejoicing which is in marked contrast to the gloom surrounding Fanny on her return to Mansfield. Fanny's jubilation seems somewhat callous; Emma's seems entirely appropriate.

The new society is achieved in *Mansfield Park* through an expulsion of scapegoats, some of whom seem more attractive, in certain respects, than the hero and heroine. In *Emma,* there is no need for a ritual of expulsion. Emma, who has much in common with the spoiled children of *Mansfield Park,* is, unlike most of them, highly educable. Once she is purged of her faults, the new society becomes possible. She represents, at the end, a combination of "energy and spirits" with propriety and moral awareness which is more attractive than the sober rectitude of Fanny and Edmund.

Even in terms of its comic structure, however, the ending of *Emma* leaves something to be desired. Mr. Woodhouse retains too powerful an influence upon the novel's society. He represents, throughout, the forces opposed to comic values. He dislikes marriage, fears life, and opposes change. Like Emma, he repeats his obsessions and imposes them upon others by virtue of his position. In his presence, honesty, spontaneity, and the healthy enjoyment of life are out of the question. There is no possibility of his changing, of course; and we do not wish to see him expelled from the new society; but we would like to see his influence diminished more than it is. For a time it looks as if Emma and Knightley will not be able to marry until he dies.

The irrational law he would impose upon his daughter is circumvented by a manipulation of the plot which makes the marriage harmonize with his obsessions, but the high spirits of the last several chapters are considerably dampened by the prospect of the newlyweds having to humor Mr. Woodhouse for as long as he lives. The reader wishes for his death, and one cannot help imagining that Emma and Knightley will soon be troubled by inadmissible longings for release.

3

Different as it is in tone, *Emma* is not so much a departure from *Mansfield Park* as a variation upon its central theme. *Mansfield Park* shows the advantages of discipline, hardship, and struggle and the evils of excessive liberty and indulgence. *Emma* explores the same theme by making a spoiled child the central figure and showing how she is educated through a combination of suffering, correction, and good example.

The opening pages of the novel present Emma to us immediately as a spoiled child, long before Knightley identifies her as such. She has "lived nearly twenty-one years in the world with very little to distress or vex her." Her mother has been long dead; her father is feeble and indulgent; and, "in consequence of her sister's marriage," she has "been mistress of his house from a very early period." Miss Taylor has been her governess for sixteen years, but "the mildness of her temper [has] hardly allowed her to impose any restraint," and "the shadow of authority" has long since "passed away." Emma does "just what she like[s]" and is "directed chiefly by her own" judgment. Her "power of having . . . too much her own way" and "disposition to think a little too well of herself" are identified as the "real evils of her situation," "disadvantages" which threaten "alloy to her many enjoyments."

We are reminded of the Crawfords, with whom Emma has much in common. Like them, she has "sense and energy and spirits" (I, ii). She is well-endowed by nature, but deficient in nurture. There are crucial differences in her upbringing, however, which make her corrigible, whereas they are not. Miss

Taylor has given her principles (II, xvii). Her father's demands for care impose a kind of hardship and discipline and mold her into a dutiful daughter. Living in Highbury, she is insulated from the evils of worldliness and the contagion of corrupt examples. The dominant figure in her world is Knightley, who provides guidance, good example, and rebuke. She has " 'the assistance of all [his] endeavors to counteract the indulgence of other people' " (III, xvii).

Emma's deficiencies are, in Jane Austen's view, the fault of her nurture. Her existence has been too privileged; she has been made to feel too important; she has received too much deference and praise. She has not had to earn respect, to submit to judgment, or to acknowledge a higher authority. As a result, she lacks discipline, is indisposed to work, and fails to develop her potentialities. She is arrogant, self-important, and controlling. She overrates her capacities and is too confident of her knowledge, judgment, and perception. Because she is so accustomed to having reality arranged for her convenience, she is given to fantasizing and to assuming that things are probably as she wishes or imagines them to be. She has a weakness for flattering illusions and for people who feed her pride. She tends to avoid competition, to cut down rivals, and to evade unpleasant realizations. Her description of Mrs. Elton fits Emma herself very well: she is "a vain woman, extremely well satisfied with herself, and thinking much of her own importance . . . [who means] to shine and be very superior" (II, xiv).

There is a precise structure by which Jane Austen identifies Emma's faults and traces the progress of her education. Almost every time that Emma errs—in judgment, perception, or behavior—she is corrected by Knightley. He warns her of the impropriety of matchmaking, disapproves of her intimacy with Harriet Smith, is outraged by her objections to Robert Martin and her interference with Martin's proposal to Harriet, disagrees with her view of Harriet's matrimonial prospects, warns her against her designs on Mr. Elton, conveys his suspicions of Frank Churchill's secret relation with Jane, and rebukes her for insulting Miss Bates. On every occasion but the last Emma pridefully rejects Knightley's position. Each episode of rejection is paralleled by a later scene in which she humbly recognizes her error. She not only sees that Knightley was right, but she also recognizes the faulty attitudes and values which produced her mistake and determines to change. She is guilty, of course, of a good deal of backsliding; there are some lessons which she must be taught again and again. But the cumulative effect of these recognition scenes, with their accompanying repentances and resolutions, is to suggest a profound and lasting reformation. Her growth is manifested, moreover, in her actions. She accepts Knightley's rebuke at Box Hill immediately, and she begins to behave toward Miss Bates and Jane as Knightley has always told her she should.

The most important change in Emma, from Jane Austen's point of view, is in her attitude toward herself. The process is slow, but her overinflated ego is eventually reduced to a proper size. The movement is from pride to humility, from self-aggrandizement to self-castigation, from self-delusion to self-knowledge: "With insufferable vanity had she believed herself in the secret of everybody's destiny. She was proved to have been universally mistaken" (III, xi). Her more realistic estimate of herself is manifested not only by her repeated self-accusations, but also by her recognition of Knightley's merit and her submission to his authority: "She had often been negligent or perverse, slighting his advice, or even wilfully opposing him, insensible of half his merits, and quarreling with him because he would not acknowledge her false and insolent estimate of her own" (III, xii). Emma is driven to many of her recognitions by threatening complications; but when all difficulties are resolved and happiness is in sight, she does not revert to her former attitudes: "What had she to wish for? Nothing but to grow more worthy of him, whose intentions and judgment had been ever so superior to her own. Nothing but that the lessons of her past folly might teach her humility and circumspection in future" (III, xviii).

Emma's education is an example of moral growth through suffering. She is instructed not only by Knightley, but also by reality, which crushes her pride and forces her to abandon her delusional system. She does not accept Knightley's lessons until reality proves her to have been wrong and threatens to punish her for her errors. At first she suffers chiefly through the evils she brings upon Harriet Smith. She feels humbled and repentant and resolves to reform, but her pride and preeminence remain essentially undisturbed, and she repeats her errors. It is only when she begins to suffer on her own account that the truth sinks in and she realizes that she *must* change. Her behavior toward Miss Bates violates her own standards, as well as Knightley's, and threatens her with the loss both of his respect and of her own esteem. The prospect of Knightley's marrying Harriet Smith convinces her, as nothing else could do, how wrong she was to have neglected Jane, to have become intimate with Harriet, and to have opposed her marriage to Robert Martin. The blows to her ego, combined with the prospect of losing Knightley, cure her of her delusions of self-sufficiency. She realizes how much Knightley has always meant to her and how much she needs him now. She is no longer the prideful woman who sees marriage only as a threat to her power and preeminence.

Emma has a comic education plot. The heroine errs as a result of her faults, suffers as a result of her errors, grows as a result of her suffering, and achieves happiness as a result of her growth. (In a tragic education plot, the protagonist grows as a result of his suffering, but is destroyed as a result of his errors.) From Jane Austen's point of view, there is no reason to doubt that Emma's reformation will be permanent and complete. Every fault has been chastened, every error has been corrected, every illusion has been removed. Emma's humility of spirit and respect for Knightley's authority assure continued growth and a prevailing rectitude of heart, mind, and conduct. Her change has already been so remarkable as to earn Knightley's esteem: they " 'have every right that equal worth can give,' " he proclaims, " 'to be happy together' " (III, xvii). As Wayne Booth observes, "this will be a happy marriage because there is simply nothing left to make it anything less than perfectly happy. It fulfills every value embodied in the world of the book—with the possible exception that Emma may never learn to apply herself as she ought to her reading and her piano!"[1]

71

4

"Marriage to an intelligent, amiable, good, and attractive man is the best thing that can happen to this heroine," says Booth, "and the readers who do not experience it as such are, I am convinced, far from knowing what Jane Austen is about" *(Rhetoric,* p. 260). As he is aware, there *are* such readers:

> G. B. Stern laments, in *Speaking of Jane Austen,* "Oh, Miss Austen, it was *not* a good solution; it was a bad solution, an unhappy ending, could we see beyond the last pages of the book." Edmund Wilson predicts that Emma will find a new protégée like Harriet, since she has not been cured of her inclination to "infatuations with women." Marvin Mudrick even more emphatically rejects Jane Austen's explicit rhetoric; he believes that Emma is still a "confirmed exploiter," and for him the ending must be read as ironic. (P. 259)

The mistakes of these readers arise, Booth feels, from looking "at Emma and Knightley as real people." From this perspective, he acknowledges, the "ending will seem false"; but for him this is an inadmissible perspective.

It is quite possible, it seems to me, both to experience *Emma* from Jane Austen's point of view, to know what she thinks she is doing, and to recognize that the novel which she has actually created does not always support her intentions. If we are guided wholly by her rhetoric, we will miss a large part of her achievement and fail to recover some of her deepest intuitions. Instead of ruling out responses which are in conflict with the author's explicit rhetoric, it may be more fruitful to ask if there is not something in the novel—unperceived, perhaps, by the author—to which these critics are reacting.

What these critics see, without articulating it precisely, is that Emma is more than an aesthetic and an illustrative character. She is an imagined human being whose problems have deep psychological sources. The experience she undergoes does not seem sufficient to cure her, and the conditions of her marriage do not seem to promise the degree of happiness which the ending predicts. Booth is right about Jane Austen's intentions. Those who object to the ending have a correct intuition about the persistence of Emma's problems and the incompleteness of the novel's resolution. Both positions are supported by the text. The conflict between them is sponsored not only by differing critical perspectives, but also by internal disparities between rhetoric and mimesis. To understand these disparities properly we must give as much attention to the analysis of Emma's character and development as critics have hitherto given to Jane Austen's view of these phenomena. By seeing Emma as a creation inside a creation, we shall at once account for the novel's inner tensions and enhance our appreciation of Jane Austen's genius in mimetic characterization.

From a psychological point of view, *Emma* is the story of a young woman with both narcissistic and perfectionistic trends which have been induced by her early environment.[2] She has great pride in her superior position and abilities and in her high moral standards. Her need to reinforce and to protect this pride leads her to be domineering toward her subordinates, competitive toward her rivals, and dutiful toward those for whom she feels a sense of responsibility. She suffers inner conflict when she is supposed to be good to her competitors or when she harms (or is in danger of harming) those whom she is supposed to protect. These conflicts produce psychological distress which ranges from mild discomfort to intense self-hate. Her defensive strategies lead her to misconstructions of reality and to moral errors. The recognition of her mistakes and of their potentially serious consequences crushes her pride and generates feelings of anxiety and self-contempt. No longer confident of her own preeminence and rectitude, she transfers her pride to Knightley and restores her position by submitting to and possessing him. This change signifies not maturation, but the substitution of a new defensive strategy for the ones which have collapsed. Her relation to her father, which has all along prevented her from becoming a mature woman, remains essentially unchanged at the end. She cannot marry Knightley until a twist in the plot removes all parental opposition.

The narcissistic person "is often gifted beyond average, early and easily won distinctions, and sometimes was the favored and admired child" *(NHG,* p. 194). He is "driven by the need for . . . self-aggrandizement or for being on top" *(NHG,* p.

192). He gains the necessary feeling of mastery not by work or vindictive triumphs, but by "self-admiration and the exercise of charm" *(NHG,* p. 212). Narcissism means "being 'in love with one's idealized image' " (*NHG,* p. 194). The narcissistic person "*is* his idealized self and seems to adore it. This . . . gives him the buoyancy or the resiliency entirely lacking in the other groups" (my italics). Beneath his "belief in his greatness and uniqueness," however, there lurks a nagging insecurity: "He may speak incessantly of his exploits or of his wonderful qualities and needs endless confirmation of his estimate of himself in the form of admiration and devotion." His solution tends to divorce him from reality and thereby makes him highly vulnerable: "His plans are often too expansive. He does not reckon with limitations. He overrates his capacities" *(NHG,* p. 195). As a result, "failures occur easily. Up to a point his resilience gives him a capacity to bounce, but . . . repeated failures . . . may crush him altogether. The self-hate and self-contempt, successfully held in abeyance otherwise, may then operate in full force" *(NHG,* p. 195). The applicability of this description to Emma is striking.

Emma's childhood situation is, like Fanny Price's, unhealthy, but to a lesser degree and in a different way. Unlike Fanny, Emma is well-gratified in many of her basic needs. She is socially secure. She feels loved, has a sense of belonging, and is treated with consideration and respect. She seems to have an abundance of self-esteem. In truth, however, her self-esteem is shaky; and a close examination of her behavior shows that she is busily engaged in warding off threats and in seeking reassurance.

Emma is insecure in her self-esteem because almost everything in her situation has contributed to the formation of an unrealistic self-image. She is the favored child, the cleverest member of the family, the mistress of Hartfield, the first lady of Highbury. Her father praises her constantly, almost everyone treats her deferentially, and her governess devotes "all her powers to attach and amuse" her, adapting herself to Emma's "every pleasure, every scheme" (I, i). All of this inflates Emma's sense of her own power, ability, and importance, while making it unnecessary for her to earn her rewards through effort and achievement. As a result, she makes great claims for herself; but she lacks real self-confidence, which could have come only from testing herself against reality and knowing that she had deserved whatever she receives in the way of praise and respect. Emma identifies with her idealized image, which in her case is not a compensation for low self-esteem but is a product of the inflated estimate of herself which she receives from others. She loves her proud self, feels little need to change, and exuberantly plays out her role. Consciously she has few doubts, but unconsciously she is plagued by anxieties which manifest themselves in her behavior.

Emma's insecurity is revealed in part by the frequent defensiveness of her behavior. She is competitive toward women like Jane Fairfax and Mrs. Elton, who threaten her position as favored child or first lady of Highbury. Jane is her chief rival for the attention and acclaim of the neighborhood; and her accomplishments make Emma uncomfortably aware of the disparity between her own promise and her performance, between other people's praise of her playing and its true worth. Emma's attitudes toward Jane have many of the characteristics of sibling rivalry. She hates to hear Jane praised, and she is hostile toward Miss Bates partly because the old woman is always talking of her niece. Emma dislikes Jane's presence in the neighborhood, is unfriendly to her when she is there, and cuts Jane down by imagining things to her disadvantage and making sport of her with Frank Churchill. She defends her pride, in other words, by either avoiding Jane or belittling her. Since her moral standards tell her that she *should* be a friend to Jane, she is never comfortable with her own behavior; and she needs to assuage her guilt by periodic self-criticism and resolutions to reform.

The fact that we are meant to share Emma's estimate of Mrs. Elton may obscure our perception that Emma is threatened by this woman who is, in many respects, a vulgar version of herself. Both women seek praise, wish to control others, and need to be recognized as first in importance. When Mrs. Elton's status as a newly married woman gives her precedence over Emma, Emma is genuinely disturbed and thinks that it might be worthwhile, after all, to consider marriage. The competition with Mrs. Elton is not enough, of course, to propel her into marrying; but we should take her discomfort seriously as an indication of the importance which being first has for Emma. If she were more secure, she would not be so jealous of petty distinctions. Emma is severely critical of Mrs. Elton not only because the latter deserves it, but also because she has a powerful need to put down a woman whom she experiences as a rival.

Emma is outraged and indignant when Mrs. Elton offers to sponsor her in Bath by providing an introduction to a friend of hers there: "The dignity of Miss Woodhouse, of Hartfield, was sunk indeed!" (II, xiv). She has a similar reaction, though far more intense, when Mr. Elton proposes marriage: ". . . that he . . . should suppose himself her equal in connection or mind! . . . and be so blind . . . as to fancy himself showing no presumption in addressing her!—It was most provoking" (I, xvi). Emma is "insulted by his hopes" because, by showing that he does not regard her as inestimably above him, they threaten to bring her down from the heights of her illusory grandeur. In order to restore her pride, she carefully rehearses in her own mind all the grounds of her superiority: "Perhaps it was not fair to expect him to feel how very much he was her inferior in talent, and all the elegancies of mind. The very want of such equality might prevent his perception of it; but he must know that in fortune and consequence she was greatly his superior. He must know that the Woodhouses . . . [were] the younger branch of a very ancient family—and that the Eltons were nobody." Emma is so jealous of her dignity, so angry when it is challenged, and so eager to reaffirm it, because she lives largely for the gratification of her pride, which is highly vulnerable. Mr. Elton's proposal, like Mrs. Elton's patronage, is completely incompatible with her idealized image of herself.

Emma's rivalry with Knightley is different from those which we have so far examined. Each of her competitors tends to threaten a different aspect of her idealized image, a different set of claims. She acknowledges Donwell to be the equal of Hartfield in consequence and takes pride in her sister's connection with the Knightleys. She is the first lady of Highbury, and George Knightley is the first gentleman. Her rivalry with Knightley is in the areas of perception and judgment. Since he is a man, older, much respected, and authoritative in manner, she is somewhat in awe of him; but, perhaps for that very reason, she clings to a belief that, on some matters at least, she is his superior in insight and discrimination. When they disagree, she tenaciously maintains her own point of view. She longs for vindictive triumphs, for events to prove her right; but it is invariably he who is shown to have been correct. After a series of mortifications, her pride is broken; and she submits herself entirely to Knightley's guidance.

Emma's insecurity is revealed not only by her competitiveness, but also by her pursuit of reassurance. Not only does she avoid people who threaten her, but she also seeks out the company of those who feed her pride. Harriet, Mrs. Weston, and Mr. Woodhouse constitute her claque; in their presence she can be assured of admiration and applause. The mental deficiencies of Harriet and her father disturb Emma at times, but usually she welcomes them as a confirmation of her own superiority. Mrs. Weston is intelligent, but deferential. This combination makes her an excellent source of reinforcement, and it is easy to understand why Emma is so often at Randalls. Critical of almost everyone and contemptuous of many, Emma tends to ignore the faults and to overrate the virtues of this trio. To deprecate them would diminish the value of their exaltation of herself.

Emma's scheming should be seen as, in part at least, an expression of her need for reassurance. It is an effort to repeat the triumphs of her childhood; it is an aspect of her search for glory. The search for glory is usually compensatory in nature. The individual has been made to feel weak, worthless, and, in various ways, inferior. He compensates for all this by creating, with the help of his imagination, an idealized image which raises him above others; and he embarks upon the project of actualizing his idealized image, of attaining in reality the glory which he feels he deserves and which he has already experienced in imagination. Emma's case is different. In this, as in all her defensive strivings, she seeks not to make up for childhood deprivations, but to hold onto the exalted status which she has already been accorded. She is, at the beginning of the novel, already in possession of her glory. Her project is not so much to actualize her idealized image as to find ways of maintaining it.

This presents a considerable difficulty. What is Emma to do? What adult role is she to play? She cannot rely upon her "accomplishments" to provide confirmation, for she has never attained excellence. One reason for this, as we have seen, is that she has never had to prove herself; she has always been surrounded by praise. Another reason, I suspect, is that she protects her pride by leaving her projects unfinished and doing less than she can. She cannot risk being judged on her best effort. It is safer to remain a promising but undisciplined child who could do great things if she tried. In the presence of so challenging a competitor as Jane Fairfax, her lack of effort provides an excuse for not being first in accomplishments.

Emma could seek to reaffirm her glory through a grand marriage. But marriage, she feels, has little to offer: " 'Fortune I do not want; consequence I do not want: I believe few married women are half as much mistress of their husband's house, as I am of Hartfield; and never, never could I expect to be so truly beloved and important; so always first and always right in any man's eyes as I am in my father's' " (I, x). Marriage presents itself to Emma less as an opportunity for fulfillment than as a threat. She would have to give up her domestic power and her status as the favored child. There are additional reasons, as we shall see, for her rejection of marriage. The question remains then: what is Emma to do? How is she to preserve the domestic situation which is so necessary to her pride and at the same time discover an activity, suitable to her years, which will maintain the sense of mastery and mental superiority that has been fostered by her experience as a spoiled child?

Emma's solution is to live through other people, to imagine their destinies, and to manage their lives. She will be a matchmaker. As the novel opens, she has just had a great success: Miss Taylor has married, and Emma " 'made the match' " herself (I, i). When Mr. Woodhouse asks her not to make any more matches, Emma promises to make none for herself, " 'but I must, indeed, for other people. It is the greatest amusement in the world. And after such success you know!' " This project has given her an occupation and a sense of direction for four years, and the happy result confirms her sense of power and perspicacity. But the completion of her project and the departure of

Miss Taylor leave a void in her life. It is soon filled by Harriet Smith who has, like Miss Taylor, the compliant disposition which Emma likes in other people. Emma will be Harriet's sponsor, her mentor. Everything that Harriet becomes she will owe to Emma. Her improvement, her triumphs, and, finally, her superior marriage will all redound to the glory of her maker. It is no wonder that Emma does not want Harriet to marry Robert Martin. This would deprive her of occupation and deny her a splendid opportunity to exercise her powers.

Emma's plans for Harriet and her plans for Mr. Elton quickly coalesce. She has far too much pride invested in the success of her project and far too much confidence in her powers of judgment and control to perceive that she is encouraging Mr. Elton and that it is she, and not Harriet, who is his object. As she herself comes to see, she takes "up the idea . . . and [makes] everything bend to it" (I, xvi). When she brings Harriet and Elton together in the Vicarage, she feels, "for half a minute, . . . the glory of having schemed successfully"; but Elton, of course, does not "come to the point" (I, x). His proposal to her instead is such a blow, not only because it insults her dignity, but also because it deprives her of glory, challenges her sense of mastery, and calls into question the superiority of her "Understanding." His scorn of Harriet, in whom she has now invested her pride, is an offense to herself. The bitterness of this experience makes her wish to avoid a repetition, and she resolves "to do such things no more" (I, xvi).

Emma is far too resilient, of course, to be permanently discouraged by a single setback. In addition, her unconscious compulsions continue to operate. Driven by her needs to protect her pride and to reaffirm her idealized image, she fastens upon one ill-conceived idea after another and makes everything bend to it. Repeated disillusionments and failures eventually puncture her narcissism and produce a change in her behavior, the exact meaning of which I shall discuss later.

Emma needs not only to be great, but also to be perfectly good. Her expansiveness takes the form not only of narcissism, but of perfectionism as well. The perfectionistic person "identifies himself with his standards" and makes "strenuous efforts to

79

measure up to his shoulds by fulfilling duties and obligations, by polite and orderly manners" *(NHG,* p. 196). He "feels superior because of his high standards . . . and on this basis looks down on others." He hides his "arrogant contempt of others," however, "because his very standards prohibit such 'irregular' feelings." He defends his pride by equating "standards and actualities—*knowing* about moral values and *being* a good person," by denying his own deficiencies, and by externalizing his self-condemnation. He is harsh upon others when they fall below his standards or display failings which he cannot afford to recognize in himself. His pride in his good qualities is intense but vulnerable. It tends to be broken by misfortune and by "his recognition of an error or failure of his own making" *(NHG,* p. 197). When he realizes "his own fallibility," "self-effacing trends and undiluted self-hate, kept in check successfully hitherto, then may come to the fore."

It is Emma's perfectionistic tendencies which gain her a large measure of approval from Jane Austen even before her pride is broken near the end, for the author has strong perfectionistic elements in her own personality. Emma is no callous manipulator. Her resolution, after the Elton affair, "to do such things no more" is motivated in part by feelings of guilt and concern for the harm she has done to Harriet. She has a strong sense of duty toward her father, her guests, her friends and dependents, and the poor of the neighborhood. We often see her working very hard to perform her various roles in an exemplary fashion. When she lives up to her standards, she experiences a self-approbation which often manifests itself in high spirits and gracious behavior. When she is conscious of failure, she is always distressed, sometimes exceedingly; and she usually attempts to remedy the situation as far as she is able.

Emma's perfectionism demands not only that she be good, but also that she be the ideal lady, the model of elegance, good taste, and fine manners. She tends to measure everyone on a scale of refinement and to be contemptuous of those who fall below her own standards. Her criticism of others is a reaffirmation of her own superiority.

Emma's perfectionism, like her narcissism, is induced not by deprivation, but by an excess of approbation. Having always been told that she is perfect, and having derived immense satisfaction from such praise, Emma is under strong pressure to live up to this exalted image of herself. Her narcissism gives rise to a great many claims; she experiences her perfectionism largely as shoulds. She may not work at her piano and her painting, but she does her best to be perfect in her moral relations. The chief threat to her self-regard is Knightley, whose standards are even higher than her own and who has a kind of authority because of his social position and the similarity of his character structure. When subjected to his criticisms, Emma must either defend her pride or be crushed.

Emma's perfectionism manifests itself in its most striking and compulsive form in her relationship with her father. It derives, indeed, chiefly from their pathological interaction. Emma may seem to be in control of the situation at Hartfield; but she manages her father—and, indeed, her own life—only in small matters It is Mr. Woodhouse who dictates the life style of Hartfield and who determines the possibilities of Emma's existence. He presents himself as a man on the verge of extinction who can be kept alive and in tolerable comfort only by the rigid observance of his wishes. He manipulates Emma through a combination of dependency and praise. She receives from him two complementary messages. The first is that if she does not cater to his weakness and respect his obsessions, he will become nervous and depressed and may, indeed, die. The second is that she is wonderful for being so good to him. The result, for Emma, is that she cannot do anything that will disturb her father. If she did, she would have to take the risk of destroying him and of losing her status as the perfect daughter. The resulting guilt and shame would be unbearable.

Jane Austen depicts Emma's relation with her father in brilliant mimetic detail, but she seems quite blind to its destructiveness and to the compulsive nature of Emma's "goodness." She is indulgent toward Mr. Woodhouse, softens his role as a blocking force, and approves of Emma's hypersensitivity to his needs and wishes. She does not see that Emma is severely constrained by his embeddedness and that she is forced by the combination of his praise and demands into a self-alienated development. Emma is not free to feel her own feelings and to consult her own wishes. She is compelled, much of the time, to repress her resentment, to disguise her feelings, and to act a part. In her father's presence, her lack of spontaneity, congruity, and transparence is striking and nearly complete.

I do not mean to suggest that Emma's acting is for her father only. She is motivated in almost all of her relationships by her need to maintain the various components of her idealized image. As a result, she is almost always, to some extent, insincere. The burdensomeness of this becomes clear when she begins to look forward to a relatively frank relationship with Knightley. His having seen through her pretenses is in some ways a relief. She can abandon her pride and, with it, the necessity of playing a role. Mr. Woodhouse remains, however; and it is not pleasant to imagine the constant hard labor of pretending which living with him will entail.

As we have seen, Emma's narcissism is partly responsible for her attitude toward marriage, which seems to her a state which will threaten rather than enhance her power and preeminence. The chief reason for her lack of interest in marriage, however, is that it is incompatible with her relation to her father. " 'I must see somebody very superior to any one I have seen yet,' " she tells Harriet, " 'to be tempted . . . and I do *not* wish to see any such person. I would rather not be tempted' " (I, x). If she were to be tempted, she would experience, as she knows, a painful conflict. In order to accept a husband, she would have, it must seem, to kill her father and to become the worst instead of the best of daughters.

Even when she realizes that Knightley must marry no one else, she still does not want him to marry her: "Marriage, in fact, would not do for her. It would be incompatible with what she owed to her father, and with what she felt for him. Nothing should separate her from her father. She would not marry, even if she were asked by Mr. Knightley" (III, xii). After Knightly proposes, "a very short parley with her own heart produced the most solemn resolution of never quitting her father.—She even wept over the idea of it, as a sin of thought. While he lived, it must be only an engagement . . . " (III, xiv).

The conflict in which she finds herself because of her relationship with her father produces a strong tendency toward detachment in Emma. The most important feelings and activities for a woman of her age and culture are simply inadmissible to her. In order to avoid guilt and conflict she represses her sexual nature and renounces her aspirations for an adult, autonomous, fruitful existence. " 'Were I to fall in love,' " she tells Harriet, " 'indeed, it would be a different thing! But I have never been in love: it is not my way or nature; and I do not think I ever shall' " (I, x). As " 'objects for the affections,' " she will have her sister's children. She will be Aunt Emma! There will be enough children " 'for every hope and every fear; and though my attachment to none can equal that of a parent, it suits my ideas of comfort better than what is warmer and blinder.' " There is a reserve, even a frigidity about Emma which is entirely explicable in the light of her bond with her father. Since all warm and intimate relationships threaten that bond, Emma cannot allow herself to experience even the desire for them, which would be a sin of thought, but must settle for what is cooler and more comfortable. She renounces not only her sexual and maternal feelings, but also the active living of her own life. She becomes an onlooker. She lives vicariously, through protégées and other people's marriages.

Emma *is* attracted to the idea of being courted by Frank Churchill, but she never wishes their relationship to become serious. What transpires between them is mostly in her imagination (though Frank, for his own purposes, is attentive); and she arranges everything, his feelings and her own, to suit her various psychological needs. Her "imagination" gives him "the distinguished honour . . . if not of being really in love with her, of being at least very near it, and saved only by her own indifference" (II, vii). It is important for her to feel that she has him in her power, that he would be hers if she wished it; but "her resolution . . . of never marrying" requires that she be indifferent and that his passion not be so strong as to produce painful scenes and a disappointment which would expose her to reproach. Eventually she comes to feel that she, too, is in love, but only a little: " 'I must be in love; I should be the oddest creature in the world if I were not—for a few weeks at least' " (II, xii). Emma's detachment has evidently made her feel odd; being in love assures her that she is a normal woman. She is pleased, however, to feel no temptation to accept nis proposal:

> the conclusion of every imaginary declaration on his side was that she *refused him*. Their affection was always to subside into friendship. Every thing tender and charming was to mark their parting; but still they were to part. When she became sensible of this, it struck her that she could not be very much in love; for in spite of her previous and fixed determination never to quit her father, never to marry, a strong attachment certainly must produce more of a struggle than she could forsee in her own feelings . . . . "I do suspect that he is not really necessary to my happiness. So much the better . . . . I am quite enough in love. I should be sorry to be more." (II, xiii)

Everything is working out for Emma in the best possible way. She imagines Frank to be in love with her, which satisfies her pride. She feels that she is in love with him, which attests to her normality, but not so much that she will be tempted to sins, either of thought or of deed, against her father. Having been in love, moreover, gives her a feeling of security for the future: " 'I shall do very well again after a little while—and then, it will be a good thing over; for they say everybody is in love once in their lives, and I shall have been let off easily' " (II, xiii). Apparently, Emma has been afraid of love as overwhelming passion which would throw her into painful inner conflict. Having had a mild case of the disease, to which everyone, it seems, is subject, she feels safe against its more virulent forms. Frank's absence cools her completely; and when she hears of his return, she is determined not "to have her own affections entangled again" (III, i). She is afraid that his feelings might produce "a crisis, an event, a something to alter her present composed and tranquil state" and is relieved to find him decidedly less attentive than before. There is little reason to believe, I might add, that Emma has been in love with Frank at all. Her feelings have been governed by conventional expectations and by her various defensive needs.

The change in Emma is precipitated largely by two events: the Box Hill episode and the discovery that Harriet hopes to marry Knightley. To appreciate the significance of the Box Hill episode, it is important to understand three things: (1) why Emma insults Miss Bates, (2) why, after Knightley's rebuke, she is so depressed, and (3) what effect this experience has upon her feelings toward Knightley.

Emma's insult has been foreshadowed earlier in the novel. She displays an aversion toward Miss Bates throughout and mocks or disparages her many times behind her back. Her attitude toward Miss Bates has a number of sources. She resents her constant praise of Jane; she has a "horror . . . of falling in with the second rate and third rate of Highbury, who were calling on [her] for ever" (II, i); and she finds Miss Bates " 'too good natured and too silly' " to suit her (I, x). Miss Bates is a poor spinster with a mother to care for who secures the charity and affection of her neighbors by a strict course of self-effacing behavior. She has "universal good-will" and a "contented temper" (I, iii). She approves of everything without discrimination, constantly expresses her gratitude, and has nothing but praise for everyone. As Emma observes, " 'nobody is afraid of her; that is a great charm' " (I, x). As is typical of an expansive person, Emma has a good deal of disdain for such self-effacing qualities. When she encounters them in people like Mr. Woodhouse, Isabella, Mr. and Mrs. Weston, and Harriet Smith, she has strong motives for repressing her contempt. It is more easily felt toward Miss Bates. Even here, however, she is not free of discomfort. She believes, like Knightley, in noblesse oblige; and she has a continual nagging guilt about her sins of omission toward Miss Bates. She has, moreover, a self-effacing component in her own personality which leads her to honor "warmth and tenderness of heart," qualities in which she knows herself to be deficient, especially toward Miss Bates. Insofar as she makes Emma feel cold-hearted or undutiful, Miss Bates is a threatening figure. As such, she arouses in Emma guilt and hostility which are not felt by Miss Bates's more genial neighbors.

Emma's insult to Miss Bates results from the slipping out, under the cover of wit, of a contempt which she had felt frequently but which she had hitherto expressed only privately or indirectly. I have discussed so far some of the reasons for a buildup of hostility toward Miss Bates, but there is yet another source which I believe to be the chief motivation behind the insult. What Emma is saying, as her victim well understands, is that Miss Bates is exceedingly "dull" and that her "society" is "irksome" (III, vii). As Emma explains to Knightley, " 'I know there is not a better creature in the world: but you must allow, that what is good and what is ridiculous are most unfortunately blended in her.' " What Emma feels most of all toward Miss Bates is an irritability in her presence, an impatience of her silliness, a resentment at being obliged to humor this "tiresome" woman (II, i). She rebels by staying away, by thwarting Miss Bates when she can, by mocking her behind her back, and, finally, by insulting her to her face. Her reactions are fully intelligible, I believe, only when we see that Emma is discharging onto Miss Bates feelings which she has, but cannot admit, toward her father.

To a dispassionate observer, Miss Bates and Mr. Woodhouse seem much alike. Like Miss Bates, Mr. Woodhouse is "everywhere beloved for the friendliness of his heart and his amiable temper" (I, i); and, like her, he is an unfortunate blend of the good and the ridiculous. Comic as they may be when they are encountered in a book, it would be impossible to enjoy their society or to find them less than oppressive as people to live with. Emma's heart goes out to Jane Fairfax at Donwell when she thinks that her distress is because of her aunt:

> Her parting words, "Oh! Miss Woodhouse, the comfort of being sometimes alone!"—seemed to burst from an overcharged heart, and to describe somewhat of the continual endurance to be practiced by her, even toward some of those who loved her best.
>
> "Such a home, indeed! such an aunt! . . . I do pity you. And the more sensibility you betray of their just horrors, the more I shall like you." (III, vi)

Emma is mistaken about Jane, but her response indicates what her own feelings would be if she had to live with Miss Bates.

More than that, it indicates what Emma's feelings *are,* unconsciously, about having to live with her father. She cannot stand being with Miss Bates because of "the continual endurance" which she must practice toward Mr. Woodhouse. She has no patience left. What Knightley sees as Miss Bates's harmless absurdities produce in Emma an almost phobic reaction.

Because of her need to be a perfect daughter, Emma must repress any irritation with her father; but the motives for repression are not strong enough to prevent such feelings from being displaced onto Miss Bates and released, from time to time, in relatively safe ways. She can feel on Jane's behalf emotions which would be completely inadmissible if she were to experience them on her own account. Emma behaves toward her father with an unfailing grace and carefully avoids sins even of thought. Her exasperation with Miss Bates, culminating in the insult at Box Hill, betrays her unconscious feelings of oppression and hostility.

As Jane Austen makes clear through Knightley's rebuke, the insult to Miss Bates is inexcusable. Even so, Emma's reaction seems out of proportion to her offense: "Never had she felt so agitated, mortified, grieved, at any circumstance in her life . . . . She had never been so depressed" (III, vii). She cries almost all the way home, in Harriet's presence, and that evening, looking back upon the day, feels it "more to be abhorred in recollection, than any she had ever passed." Emma is so distressed because she has seriously violated her perfectionistic shoulds and can find no way to protect her pride. Knightley has reproached her before, sometimes severely; but she has always been able to maintain the correctness of her own position. Now, however, his values and her own coincide; and after a few attempts at self-defense, she cannot deny "the truth of his representation." Her depression is produced, to some extent, by the collapse of her idealized image. Her self-esteem is sinking. She feels that the "degree" of her father's "fond affection and confiding esteem" is "unmerited." She feels ashamed before Knightley, guilty toward Miss Bates, and angry with herself. How could she have behaved in this way? Her sense of the heinousness of her crime may be related to the fact that Miss Bates is partly a surrogate for her father, toward whom she has the most compulsive feelings of duty. Miss Bates's dependency and compliance are also a factor; Emma has struck a defenseless person.

Emma begins to work almost immediately at restoring her pride. While recognizing that she is not as perfect as her father thinks her to be, she takes comfort in attending to him and in reflecting upon her general conduct toward him: "As a daughter, she hoped, she was not without a heart. She hoped no one could have said to her, 'How could you have been so unfeeling to your father?' " (III, viii). She assuages her guilt toward Miss Bates by self-condemnation and a determination to reform: "She had been often remiss, her conscience told her so; remiss, perhaps, more in thought than fact; scornful, ungracious." As she pays her penitential visit, she hopes to encounter Knightley, but he does not appear. When he learns of her visit, however, he understands at once "all that had passed of good in her feelings" (III, ix). They part "thorough friends," as his manner assures her that she has "fully recovered his good opinion."

Emma is comfortable once more, but things are not as they were before. An important change has taken place in her pride system and in her relation to Knightley. The self-hate and humiliation which she has experienced as a result of her own error have made her afraid of her pride and uncertain of her ability to live up to her shoulds. As a means of self-protection, she submits to Knightley's judgment and authority. If she acts and feels as he would wish, she will be certain of maintaining both his esteem and her own. She makes him an omniscient observer of her moral life, adding in this way the fear of his judgments to her own shoulds as a motive for the repression of all unacceptable impulses. She begins not only to act, but also to feel properly toward Jane and Miss Bates. When Jane rejects her kind attentions, she is "mortified" at being "given so little credit for proper feeling, or esteemed so little worthy as a friend." But she has "the consolation of knowing that her intentions were good, and of being able to say to herself, that could Mr. Knightley have been privy to all her attempts of assisting Jane Fairfax, could he even have seen into her heart, he would not, on this occasion, have found any thing to reprove" (III, ix). Emma is still proud of her goodness, but she experiences her pride now through Knightley's imagined approval rather than through a direct identification with her idealized image.

The Box Hill episode marks the beginning, I believe, of Emma's tender feelings for Knightley. As Horney observes, an expansive person often cannot love until his pride is broken. Emma's humiliation at Knightley's hands arouses feelings of weakness, anxiety, and self-hate. She becomes dependent upon his approval to relieve these feelings and upon his reinforcement to prevent their recurrence. When Knightley hears of her visit to Miss Bates, he looks at her "with a glow of regard":

> She was warmly gratified—and in another moment still more so, by a little movement of more than common friendliness on his part.—He took her hand;— whether she had not herself made the first motion, she could not say—she might, perhaps, have rather offered it—but he took her hand, pressed it, and certainly was on the point of carrying it to his lips—when, from some fancy or other, he suddenly let it go. (III, ix)

Emma is disappointed that he did not complete the motion. There are earlier signs of Knightley's attraction to her, but this is the first instance of a tender impulse on her part toward him. Emma is not aware of the change in their relationship, but this scene prepares for the recognition which is to follow.

Emma's pride receives a devastating blow when she learns of Harriet's hopes of winning Knightley. The two things most important to her, her self-esteem and her preeminence, are severely threatened by this discovery. When Harriet indicates that Frank Churchill is not her object, Emma waits speechless and "in great terror" to learn the truth (III, xi). When all is revealed, including the fact that Harriet has some reasonable hope of a return, it darts through Emma, "with the speed of an arrow, that Mr. Knightley must marry no one but herself!" This intuition is in part a recognition of her own love and her need for his affection. It is mainly, however, a response to threat. If Knightley marries Harriet—or anyone else, for that matter—Emma will lose her position of preeminence, both as first lady of Highbury and, insofar as Knightley is in some respects a father substitute, as favored child. Now that she is "threatened with its loss," Emma discovers how much of her happiness depends "on being *first* with Mr. Knightley, first in interest and affection" (III, xii). She need not marry him, but he must not marry anyone else: "Could she be secure of that, indeed, of his never marrying at all, she believed she should be perfectly satisfied.—Let him but continue the same Mr. Knightley to her and her father . . . and her peace would be fully secured." Given her bond to her father, this would, indeed, be the best solution. What she cannot stand is the thought of Harriet being "the chosen, the first, the dearest." When Knightley proposes, Emma's earliest distinct thought is "that Harriet was nothing, that she was everything herself" (III, xiii).

The discovery of her latest mistake about Harriet is the culminating blow to Emma's pride in the superiority of her values and perceptions. Immediately following her realization that Knightley must marry no one but herself comes a recognition of her own faults. She finds every "part of her mind," other than "her affection for Mr. Knightley," to be "disgusting." Her mistakes strike her now with such "dreadful force" because they have brought upon her a real possibility of disaster. They can no longer be juggled away by an internal process of rationalization or denial, and there seems to be nothing she can do to restore her position. Her realization that Knightley has been right all along and that she could have avoided her present troubles by following his advice makes him assume all the more the aspect of an infallible authority, and she is full of remorse at her earlier impiety. She hates herself and reveres Knightley.

Knightley's proposal enables Emma to rebuild her pride. Her social position is now secure, and she has won a man who is clearly superior to the husband of her chief rival, Jane. She maintains a low estimate of herself, but at the same time she derives reassurance from the fact that so upright and discriminating a man has found her worthy of his love. Since Knightley approves of it, her self-abasement becomes a virtue in which she can take satisfaction. Her many errors of heart and head have made her profoundly distrustful of herself, but she hopes to maintain her perfection in the future by reminding herself of Knightley's superiority and her own past folly (III, xviii).

At the beginning of the novel, Emma identifies with her idealized image. Reality seems to be honoring her narcissistic claims, and she is conscious of fulfilling her perfectionistic shoulds. In the course of the action she receives a series of blows, as her schemes misfire and her perceptions and judgments are proved to have been wrong. She restores her pride in a variety of ways; but her pride system becomes more and more vulnerable as she confronts, again and again, the disparity between her idealized image and reality. The blows which she receives at Box Hill and in her interview with Harriet penetrate her defenses, crush her pride, and generate paroxysms of self-condemnation. Her anguish passes, as events prove favorable; but a significant change takes place in her pride system. She feels weak and unworthy rather than powerful and perfect, and she defends herself against the resulting self-hate and anxiety by transferring her pride to Knightley and experiencing it vicariously through him. Her needs for power and perfection remain unchanged, and she pursues them as compulsively as before, but in a different manner. She idealizes Knightley now, instead of herself, and depends upon his rectitude and preeminence to sustain her worth.

The crushing of Emma's pride and the substitution of compliant for expansive trends seem like growth to Jane Austen because of her own glorification of the self-effacing solution. But when Emma is understood psychologically, there is no reason to believe that she is moving significantly toward self-actualization. This is not to deny that Emma learns from her experiences and makes a better adaptation to her society. She discovers the independence of external reality and gains a knowledge of her inability to control it. She is forced to give up her narcissistic claims and to recognize the immorality of many of her expansive attitudes. Insofar as it made her averse to marriage, her striving for power had cut her off from any meaningful role in her society. The emergence of self-effacing trends leads her to desire marriage and qualifies her for the role of wife. At the beginning of the novel, Emma is an unusual figure in her world; by the end she has the feminine personality which was most commonly induced and most strongly approved by the society of her time.

Given Emma's psychological needs at the end, we must agree with Wayne Booth that marriage to Knightley is "the best thing that can happen to this heroine"; but if we look at it closely, the Emma-Knightley marriage seems far from ideal. The relationship is not based on mature love on the part of either member. Emma is drawn to Knightley by the needs and anxieties which arise when her pride is broken. She has been a spoiled child; now she is a chastened and compliant one who seeks safety through submission to a wise authority.

Knightley will keep her wayward impulses under control, but he will not help her to grow. He is himself a perfectionist who, unlike Emma, succeeds in living up to his own standards. He is attracted to Emma by both her perfectionism and her narcissistic pride and immaturity. He approves of her dutifulness, especially toward her father, but he also enjoys being superior to her in wisdom and maturity. Her pride arouses his competitiveness, and her faults, which give him the victory, are part of her charm. He takes pleasure in being proved right and is most impressed by Emma when she submits to his lecturing. He has found her physically attractive for a long time. The fancied competition with Frank Churchill makes him realize, perhaps unconsciously, how much he enjoys his role of mentor and how important it is to him to be *first* with Miss Woodhouse. When Emma submits to him, he must play down her deficiencies in order to maintain the value of his prize. She is the "sweetest and best of all creatures, faultless in spite of all her faults" (III, xiii). To satisfy his own pride, he needs at once to exalt Emma and to keep her inferior to him. Since she needs at once to receive his approval and to remind herself of his superiority, their relationship promises to be mutually satisfying. That does not, however, make it healthy. It is difficult to see Emma, under Knightley's tutelage, outgrowing her dependency. If she did, there might be trouble.

In one respect Emma does not change at all. She remains completely bound to her father. After Knightley's proposal, the conflict which she has always feared between love and duty confronts her, but it is quickly resolved: she determines never to quit her father, weeps over the idea as a sin of thought, and decides that "while he live[s], it must be only an engagement" (III, xiv). Her conflict is easily disposed of because she does not really have to choose between the two men: Knightley is hers, whether she marries him or not. The problem is really Knightley's. How is he to gain Emma in marriage without violating his (and her) sense of duty toward Mr. Woodhouse? The solution which he proposes is to make Hartfield his home. We are supposed to feel, with Mrs. Weston, that this involves "no sacrifice on any side worth the name" (III, xvii). Emma recognizes, however, as have many readers, "that in living constantly with her father, and in no house of his own, there would be much, very much, to be borne with" (III, xv).

Knightley's solution, involving, as it does, an insistence on marriage, makes Emma's conflict more severe. Not only has she no rational ground for opposing the union, but she also has a strong emotional need to comply with Knightley's wishes. But she knows that even with Knightley's sacrifice Mr. Woodhouse will be unhappy about her marrying. In her relations with her father, Emma has no power of self-assertion. Her need to be the perfect daughter is so compulsive that she cannot do anything, however justified, that will disturb him. She is a slave to his irrational claims. Even though Knightley is eager and Mr. Woodhouse is beginning to be resigned, Emma is paralyzed:

> Still, however, he was not happy. Nay, he appeared so much otherwise, that his daughter's courage failed. She could not bear to see him suffering, to know him fancying himself neglected; and though her understanding almost acquiesced in the assurance of both the Mr. Knightleys, that when once the event were over, his distress would be soon over too, she hesitated—she could not proceed. (III, xix)

Then Mrs. Weston's turkey coop is robbed, and the problem is resolved.

The manipulated ending is in complete accord with the laws and spirit of comedy. It saves Emma from having to make a painful choice, and it reconciles Mr. Woodhouse to the marriage. It serves Jane Austen's thematic purposes by maintaining the illusion of Emma's maturation. By arranging the world to fit Emma's defensive needs, she obscures the psychological realities which she has portrayed so vividly. She does not want us to see, nor can she afford to see consciously herself, the severity of Emma's father problem and the fact that it is unresolved.

Through Emma and through Frank Churchill, Austen dramatizes brilliantly the damaging effects of manipulation by sick, life-denying parental figures. The novel seems, at one point, to promise a thematic exploration of this problem (I, xviii); but Austen has, understandably, no wisdom to offer. All that she can propose is to follow the self-effacing (or the perfectionistic) route of doing one's duty. Frank should have stood up to Mrs. Churchill in the name of his obligation to his father. But he can only get what he wants for himself (and has a right to have) if Mrs. Churchill dies. The dilemma he faces, and the frustrations he has had to endure, account for his dishonorable behavior, which is treated (perhaps because Austen sympathizes) with a surprising mildness.

As the Knightleys' assurances indicate, Emma is not forced by her situation to suspend the marriage. It would have been perfectly moral for her to proceed, expressing all the while her love and concern for her father. His unhappiness would have passed. Jane Austen's amused tone suggests that she has some awareness of the irrationality of Emma's decision, but she seems, nevertheless, to be basically sympathetic toward her heroine's self-sacrificial behavior. She could not have had Emma behave differently, of course. Emma behaves as she must. But it was within the power of her rhetoric, if she had had a clear enough vision, to suggest the destructiveness of Emma's solution and the preferability of the Knightleys' alternative. As we have seen, Emma is in this instance saved from the consequences of her psychological problems by authorial manipulation of the plot. Form and theme work well together here. The comic action accords with the picture of the world which accompanies the self-effacing solution. Reality is antagonistic to Emma's wishes as long as she is proud. When she becomes humble and unselfish, fortune turns in her favor. Virtue is rewarded.

It is difficult to say whether Emma and Knightley have (theoretically) any acceptable alternative to living at Hartfield. As Jane Austen presents the situation, it is unthinkable either for Emma to leave her father or for Mr. Woodhouse to move to Donwell. Either course, we are made to feel, would result in his death. The only solution which the author can sanction is to have Emma and Knightley submit to Mr. Woodhouse's claims, to sacrifice their autonomy, and to live a life of "continual endurance." This may be, in fact, the only way of reconciling the demands of morality with the actualities of the situation; but, as some readers have felt, it is hardly a happy ending. Since the death of Mr. Woodhouse is the only possible source of relief, the reader is left wishing for it, and imagining the suppressed impatience of Emma and Knightley, at the end of the novel. Emma's oversolicitude about her father may well be, in fact, a defense against unconscious desires for his disappearance. The only way she can remain free of guilt when he dies is to hover about him, protecting him from every disturbing influence.

Emma Woodhouse and Fanny Price are, for the most part, opposite psychological types. It is impressive that Jane Austen could enter into the inner lives of such different characters equally well. Given her own character structure, it is not surprising that Austen could judge Emma's narcissism much better than she could see the destructiveness of Fanny's self-effacing solution. She had more distance from Emma's solution, and she could identify its sources and its inadequacies with considerable precision, as she did with the spoiled children in *Mansfield Park*. Austen's combination of empathy with insight gives rise to the sympathetic mockery, so agreeable to the modern sensibility, which sets the tone for much of *Emma*. She has blind spots in *Emma*, however, just as she does in *Mansfield Park*. She overestimates the educative value of suffering and the nobility of compulsive goodness, whether it be perfectionistic or self-effacing in origin. She interprets Emma least satisfactorily toward the end, as she becomes more self-effacing; she is not sufficiently disturbed by the embeddedness of Hartfield; and she is blind to Emma's father problem, which is the source of much of her difficulty and which remains unresolved at the end.

4

Pride and Prejudice

1

Pride and Prejudice is a fantasy of expansive triumph. In this novel it is not submissive virtue but self-assertive merit which is primarily rewarded (Jane, of course, also fares well). Elizabeth gains freedom from the oppression of her family, recognition of her personal superiority, and the power and glory of a grand marriage. She is looking for the kind of happiness which comes from the gratification of an expansive pride, and she finds it. She is good enough to deserve her happiness, but she does not have to pay for it with excessive humility or self-sacrifice. The ending of *Pride and Prejudice* is relatively free of the oppressions which dampen our pleasure in *Mansfield Park* and *Emma*. The wishes which are fulfilled are less displaced in the direction of morality.

Thematically, *Pride and Prejudice* is the most complex of Jane Austen's novels, and one which is very much in accord with the spirit of comedy. In examining the relationship between the individual and society, it recognizes the importance of social considerations; but it places a heavy stress upon the desirability of attaining personal fulfillment. It is concerned with the evils which flow from a lack of proper authority (as in the Bennet household); but it is the least concerned of all the major novels with the importance of duty and submission and the value of suffering. Jane Austen's usual practice is to look at individuals from the point of view of society and to criticize those who follow their own will or who deviate from a rigid code of manners and morality. *Pride and Prejudice* tends to look at society from the point of view of the individual and to criticize those institutions, conventions, and values which hamper intercourse and obstruct happiness.

Elizabeth Bennet is Jane Austen's first great mimetic character. Her psychological traits are less extreme, and hence less obvious, than are those of Fanny and Emma; but with the understanding gained from my study of these two heroines, it will not be difficult to see Elizabeth as an imagined human being. The analysis of Emma, in particular, will help us to understand Elizabeth. Both women are expansive, both make mistakes as a consequence, and both have their pride chastened through the discovery of their errors. The process is muted, however, in *Pride and Prejudice*. Elizabeth's faults are less palpable, her mistakes are less serious, and her humiliation is less profound. Her sense of self-knowledge comes more easily, and she needs to undergo no major reorientation of her values. She is allowed to keep her aggressiveness more or less intact, a fact which sets her apart from Emma and all other Austen heroines.

The disparity between representation and interpretation is less marked in *Pride and Prejudice* than in the other novels, but still it is there. I do not find in this novel the glorification of the compliant solution which led me to quarrel with Austen's interpretation of Fanny throughout and of Emma at the end of her story. The problem here is different. Jane Austen has less distance from Elizabeth's expansiveness than she has from Emma's. As a result, she misinterprets Elizabeth's motives for wanting to marry Darcy and the nature of their union. She understands Elizabeth best in the sequences preceding Darcy's letter, but even here she does not seem to be fully aware of the degree to which Elizabeth's behavior is dictated by defensive needs. I shall discuss these matters in the course of analyzing Elizabeth's psychology. But first let us look at the larger creation of which Elizabeth is a part.

2

Our chief concern in *Pride and Prejudice* is, of course, Elizabeth's search for happiness. Elizabeth's plight is what one imagines Jane Austen's to have been: she must find a man who is at least her equal in intelligence and sensitivity, who can give her an appropriate social and economic position, and who does not object to making a disadvantageous alliance. Mr. Collins, Wickham, and Colonel Fitzwilliam are all ruled out for one or another of these reasons. The only potentially suitable mate is Darcy, but at the time of his first proposal Elizabeth neither likes nor respects him. Since she sees marriage primarily as a means to personal happiness, this is an enormous obstacle. What the comic action requires from this point on is for Elizabeth to discover her mistakes about Darcy and to change her view of him accordingly, for Darcy himself to change in such a way as to overcome Elizabeth's remaining objections, and for their changes in character and sentiment to be somehow communicated to each other.

The obstacles to Elizabeth's marriage with Darcy are partly external and partly within each of the protagonists. As soon as Darcy finds himself attracted to Elizabeth, he begins to experience inner conflict. He admires Elizabeth for her personal qualities, but he feels that it would be demeaning to connect himself with her family. When love conquers his scruples, he proposes, but in such a way as to offend Elizabeth's dignity; and she rebukes him for his ungentlemanlike behavior. This rebuke from someone whom he respects chastens his pride and leads him to see the selfishness and snobbery of his behavior. The obstacles within Darcy have now been removed, but an external blocking force remains: the difficulty of communicating his change to Elizabeth and of discovering her sentiments. Lydia's elopement and Lady Catherine's interference are threatening only from Elizabeth's point of view (to which the reader is largely confined). In reality they are favorable to the comic resolution. Darcy's intervention on Lydia's behalf increases Elizabeth's gratitude and esteem and gives her reason to hope that he loves her still, while Elizabeth's defiance of Lady Catherine (which is duly reported) encourages Darcy to risk a second proposal.

The major obstacle to the marriage is, of course, Elizabeth's dislike of Darcy. The central action of the novel is the evolution of that dislike, its gradual softening after Darcy's first proposal, and the emergence of Elizabeth's desire for the marriage during her visit to Pemberley. "The action of comedy," says Frye, "is not unlike the action of a lawsuit, in which the plaintiff and defendant construct different versions of the same situation, one finally being judged as real and the other as illusory" *(AC,* p. 166). The movement is from *pistis* (opinion) to *gnosis* (proof). This is a perfect description of *Pride and Prejudice.* Elizabeth and Wickham are the plaintiffs and Darcy is the defendant. Because Darcy injures her pride, Elizabeth is disposed to believe Wickham's false testimony against him. It is appropriate that critics have noted the legalistic tone of Darcy's letter; it is his case for the defense.

The dispelling of illusion involves more than Elizabeth's learning the true story of Darcy and Wickham. She must recognize that Jane had given no clear sign of her love for Bingley, and she must acknowledge the justice of Darcy's reservations about an alliance, for either himself or Bingley, with the Bennet family. She must discover the extent of her own blindness and become more humble about her insight and objectivity. She must learn more about Darcy's character than she could ever discover from the superficial contact of social intercourse. And she must take, finally, a less romantic view of marriage and come to see gratitude and esteem as sound bases of a happy union.

The ending of *Pride and Prejudice* provides many of the satisfactions which we associate with the action of comedy. In the marriage of Jane and Bingley we have the triumph of romantic love over social obstacles and the removal of the

threat which hangs over the Bennet women in the form of the
irrational law of entail. Although the marriage of Elizabeth and
Darcy is less romantically gratifying, it establishes a new society
which becomes normative for the world of the novel and which
seems to assure Elizabeth of a substantial and lasting happiness.
As Frye observes, *pistis* and *gnosis* correspond " to the usurping
and the desirable societies respectively" *(AC,* p. 166). The desirable society is represented not only by Pemberley, as opposed
to Longbourn, but also by the inner qualities of Elizabeth and
Darcy, by their clear-sightedness and maturity as opposed to
their earlier pride and prejudice. Their marriage will prosper
because it is based upon a real understanding of themselves and
each other and upon a proper combination of values. The Jane-
Bingley relationship may be more passionately intense, but it is
presented as a happy accident. Fortunately for themselves, Jane
and Bingley are what they appear to be. The experience of Mr.
Bennet with his wife and of Elizabeth with Wickham and Darcy
suggests, however, that appearances are in general a poor guide
in the choice of a mate. Neither Jane's good fortune nor Charlotte's cynicism are to be taken as normative. The well-
grounded relationship of Elizabeth and Darcy shows that happiness is *not* entirely a matter of chance.

The new society which crystallizes around Elizabeth and
Darcy at Pemberley embodies a number of important values,
both from Elizabeth's and from the author's point of view. At
Longbourn, Elizabeth is a sensible person living in a world
composed largely of fools. There are few people whom she can
love, and even fewer whom she can respect. She is subject to the
irrationality of her mother (who likes her least of all the children) and to the embarrassments of belonging to an ill-regu-
lated family. She finds her situation at first laughable, and then
extremely frustrating. Her marriage to Darcy rescues her from
this world and places 'her in a proper setting. It signals a
geographical redistribution of characters which is much to Elizabeth's advantage. She is freed from her mother's presence, but
she retains the society of her father, who visits often. Jane and
Bingley settle nearby, but Lydia and Wickham are excluded
from Pemberley. They are cared for by Jane and Bingley,
however, which maintains the mood of comic inclusion; and

Elizabeth sends them money. Georgiana has "the highest opinion in the world of Elizabeth," who is very fond of her; and Miss Bingley pays "off every arrear of civility" (III, xix). A reconciliation is even effected with Lady Catherine, but it is hard to imagine that she will be a frequent guest. With the Gardiners, however, Elizabeth and Darcy are "always on the most intimate terms." At the end, Elizabeth is no longer an anomaly in her world. She is surrounded by people whom she likes and who appreciate her.

The shift from Longbourn to Pemberley represents a considerable improvement not only from a social but also from a moral point of view. There is a lack of proper authority and of rational guidance at Longburn, where the tone is set by Mrs. Bennet and her youngest daughter. The life of Pemberley is regulated by Fitzwilliam Darcy. Mr. Bennet has power when he chooses to use it, but in general he has abandoned his paternal responsibility. His daughters are allowed to be idle and frivolous if they wish. Little effort is made either to form their characters or to correct their manners. Instruction is available to those who desire it, but there is no governess, no supervision, no plan of education. The nearly disastrous affair of Lydia and Wickham is a direct consequence of Mr. Bennet's abdication. Significantly, there is a parallel situation involving Darcy. He preserves his sister from Wickham, however, and when he feels that he is at fault for not having exposed Wickham's character, he intervenes on behalf of the Bennets, playing the moral and economic roles which properly belong to Lydia's father. Thus, when he becomes leader of the new society, we feel that a state of anarchy has passed and that proper authority has at last been established. The improvement of Kitty and the respectfulness of Georgiana enhance this impression. Darcy's sobriety has its limitations, but it is far better than the levity of Longbourn.

One important quality of the ending which I have not yet discussed is the strong sense of triumph it communicates to the reader. Elizabeth makes a grand marriage, one which vindicates her worth and carries with it all of the glories so vulgarly celebrated by her mother: " 'And is it really true? Oh! my sweetest Lizzy! how rich and how great you will be! What pin money, what jewels, what carriages you will have! Jane's is nothing to it—nothing at all. I am so pleased—so happy. . . . Dear, dear Lizzy. A house in town! Everything that is charming! . . . Ten thousand a year!' " (III, xvii). Fitzwilliam Darcy is one of the most eligible men in England, and marriage to him confers upon Elizabeth a dreamlike elevation in power, wealth, and status. She will be mistress of Pemberley!

Elizabeth is not indifferent to these things. After the first proposal she is flattered at having received an offer from the great Mr. Darcy; and the sight of Pemberley really does, I believe, arouse her desire for a renewal of his attentions. We share the Gardiner's sense of excitement when Darcy behaves so gallantly to Elizabeth; and as soon as Elizabeth begins to want the marriage, we support her strongly. When obstacles arise, the novel becomes, for the first time, fraught with suspense. We want so much for Elizabeth to get her man that the issue of their personal compatibility subsides in importance. What matters is that he should still desire her, and we read hurriedly to discover favorable evidence. He had had to struggle with himself before his first proposal. Will not the disgrace of Lydia, the connection now with Wickham, and the opposition of Lady Catherine combine with his injured pride to prevent a second? His obliviousness to these difficulties is a great tribute to Elizabeth. She has the triumph not only of making a grand marriage and of being delivered from Longbourn, but also of being most highly valued.

This is, indeed, a happy ending. Nothing is left to be desired. There is even evidence on the last page that, with his wife at least, Darcy unbends. Georgiana often listens with "astonishment" to Elizabeth's "lively, sportive manner of talking to her brother" and sees him now "the object of open pleasantry." Elizabeth's manner with her husband suggests a more equal relationship than Emma has with Knightley. It would be unthinkable, of course, in Mansfield Parsonage.

3

Pride and Prejudice is Jane Austen's most sophisticated exploration of the relationship between the individual and society. In her treatment of marriage, of manners, and of various other aspects of our personal and communal lives, she attempts to strike a delicate balance between the necessity of prudence, decorum, and social responsibility on the one hand, and the desirability of self-expression, spontaneity, and personal fulfillment on the other. She gives the institutions, values, and conventions of the established order all due respect; but she shows at the same time that they are subject to distortion and can stand in the way of happiness, sincerity, and truth. Individualism, too, has its dangers, as she is always careful to show. Her satire is directed against an excessive emphasis upon either set of considerations. Her object in this novel is to explore the possibilities of combining the requirements of social life with legitimate aspirations for personal integrity and satisfaction.

Marriage is an ideal vehicle for Jane Austen's thematic concerns. It is at once a personal relationship and a social institution, and both of its aspects are important. Austen feels that one should marry for love, for personal satisfaction, and out of a regard for the human qualities of one's partner. At the same time, one cannot ignore the socioeconomic position of the other person. Mrs. Gardiner warns Elizabeth against becoming involved with Wickham, and Elizabeth accepts her advice. Attractive as Wickham seems to be at this time, he is not an eligible mate for a woman like Elizabeth, who has almost no personal fortune and whose family lives under the threat of an entail. In a similar way, Colonel Fitzwilliam finds Elizabeth attractive; but he lets her know that he must marry a woman with money. Neither Elizabeth nor Colonel Fitzwilliam would marry *for* money, but they must hope to fall in love with someone who *has* money. They are wise to avoid emotional involvement with people who are unsuitable from a prudential point of view, however attractive they may be personally.

People cannot always fall in love where they choose, but their choice of a marriage partner should not be governed primarily by concerns for money or status. There are many examples of possible or endangered connections which illustrate the potential evil of sacrificing personal preference to social or economic considerations. Elizabeth cannot forget about the entail, but she should not marry Collins because of it.

She is tolerant of Wickham's attentions to Miss King only as long as she thinks that he might care for her. Other possible marriages which illustrate this point are those of Darcy and Lady Anne, Darcy and Miss Bingley, and Bingley and Georgiana. There is no personal attraction in any of these relationships, but the marriages are desired out of personal ambition or to enhance the wealth and status of the families. The endangered connections are those of Elizabeth with Darcy and Jane with Bingley.

It is true, as many critics have observed, that *Pride and Prejudice* evokes a vision of society as governed by the values of the marketplace. Human relations, and especially the marriage relation, are threatened by an excessive emphasis upon money and status. It should be noted, however, that this debasement of social institutions and interpersonal relationships is more of a threat and an object of satire than a triumphant reality in the world of the novel. It is exemplified more by possible and endangered connections than by actual ones, and the characters whose values are faulty either turn out to have little power or are reformed.

There is one actual marriage which is motivated solely by socioeconomic considerations—that of Charlotte and Mr. Collins. When Charlotte accepts Collins, Elizabeth feels that she has "sacrificed every better feeling to worldly advantage" (I, xxii). We are eventually made to feel, however, not that Charlotte's attitude toward marriage is correct or that she has made a happy choice, but that she has been realistic for herself and has chosen the lesser evil. Jane Austen does not blame her, and even Elizabeth becomes somewhat reconciled to her choice. Charlotte's marriage remains, nonetheless, the darkest note in the novel. This sensitive and intelligent woman has been forced by the accidents of her lot to be cynical about marriage and to prostitute herself for status and security.

Elizabeth and Darcy tend to crisscross in their attitudes toward marriage in the course of the novel. Neither begins with an extreme position: Elizabeth is somewhat to the left and Darcy somewhat to the right of center. Darcy is attracted to Elizabeth quite early, but he sees the connection as unsuitable to the dignity of his family, and he tries to regulate his feelings accordingly. He is so much in love, however, that he decides to make a social sacrifice for the sake of personal satisfaction. The problem from Elizabeth's point of view is the reverse. However magnificent her prospects as Darcy's wife, she cannot think of marrying him until she comes to care for him personally.

After being at first the chief obstacle to love, Darcy becomes the most romantic figure in the book; and he does this without losing his character as the defender of traditional values. He uses his great power in the service of both order and desire. He combats the anarchistic tendencies of Lydia and Wickham on the one hand and the tyranny of Lady Catherine on the other. He saves the Bennet family and rescues the heroine from all the sources of her distress. He marries her for love and transports her to the comfort and elegance of Pemberley.

Elizabeth has a regard for the social aspects of marriage, but she seems to represent at the outset a predominantly individualistic point of view. Her change of heart toward Darcy is profoundly influenced, however, by social considerations. She is impressed at Pemberley not only by the grandeur of the estate, but also by the importance of such a man as Darcy, who has so many dependents, and by his obligation to choose wisely in the matter of a wife. Mrs. Reynolds' description of his exemplary behavior in his many social roles impresses Elizabeth quite as much as the information that he has a good temper. Elizabeth's experiences with her father have prepared her to appreciate such evidence of responsibility. When we consider that she finds herself drawn to the idea of being Darcy's wife before her renewed contact with the man himself, we must conclude that Darcy's social attractiveness plays a large part in the awakening of her desire.

There is little doubt that Jane Austen sees the marriage of Darcy and Elizabeth as a union which will "teach the admiring multitude what connubial felicity really" is (III, x). The novel aims, through this marriage, at a resolution of the dialectic I have been examining between the social and the personal aspects of marriage. By having each of the protagonists come to appreciate and to be motivated by the other's point of view, while maintaining a concern for his own, Austen seeks to do fullest justice to both sets of values.

Pride and Prejudice is as much about manners as it is about marriage. The word "civility" occurs, in one form or another, over seventy times in the novel. It is part of a cluster of frequently recurring terms which includes "manners," "decorum," "propriety," and "politeness." Civilization is based, in part, upon the observance of proper forms of behavior. In a society of highly formal manners, such as that depicted in this novel, there is a prescribed way for each individual to behave in almost every situation of life. Socialization is the process by which the individual learns his place in the world and acquires the manners appropriate to it. Ideally, he learns not only to behave, but also to feel as he ought, so that his manners communicate his true sentiments and reflect his character. In *Pride and Prejudice,* as in all of Austen's novels, individuals tend to be judged in terms of their breeding. Those who are either under- or oversocialized are objects of satire, as are those whose manners are only a facade which hides their unscrupulous natures. In manners, as in marriage, it is necessary to strike a balance between self-expression and respect for propriety.

Lydia and Collins represent the extremes of lopsided development. Lydia is uncivilized. She is guided by her impulses, which are primitive, and her manners are atrocious. She feels and behaves improperly in every situation and continually gives pain to those around her. The characters who most closely resemble her are her mother and her aunt Philips, both of whom encourage her wildness. Darcy, Lady Catherine, and Mr. Bennet also display self-indulgence in their social behavior. Collins represents the opposite evil. He seems to be nothing but his social mask or persona. His civilities are excessive partly because they have no feeling, no personal sensitivity, behind them. He overdoes what is proper in every situation and is successful only with people who are themselves preoccupied with rituals. His closest counterpart is Sir William Lucas, whose civilities are less excessive but not much more meaningful than his. Bingley, Jane, Elizabeth, and the Gardiners represent a happy combination of feeling and form: they are at once well-bred and genuinely concerned for others. Manners such as theirs, however, can be deceptive. Wickham only appears to be what they are.

Darcy's manners are in need of adjustment. They are at once too formal and too self-indulgent. Darcy's sense of dignity is so great that he has difficulty relating to people, even his intimates, with feeling and spontaneity. Darcy's self-indulgence lies in his indifference to the feelings of those who are not his equals or intimates. His "manners . . . [are] well-bred," but he will not trouble himself to be friendly, and he continually gives offence (I, vi). His faulty manners result from a flaw in his character. He changes for the better in both feeling and behavior as a consequence of Elizabeth's refusal, which forces him into self-examination: " 'I was spoiled by my parents, who . . . allowed, encouraged, almost taught me to be selfish and overbearing, to care for none beyond my own family circle, to think meanly of all the rest of the world' " (III, xvi).

It is Elizabeth who achieves the most delicate balance between the requirements of self and of society. Her manners are easy and playful, but she takes serious things seriously and is careful of the feelings of others. She does not always say what she thinks, but she knows her own mind, and she tries not to mislead or to be forced into a false position by the demands of the occasion. Upon her departure from Hunsford, while Collins engages in a ceremonious leave-taking, Elizabeth tries "to unite civility and truth in a few short sentences" (II, xv). A certain amount of hypocrisy is built into the system, of course. The well-bred person cannot be expected to like or to respect everyone he meets, but he is expected to behave in a gracious way. Elizabeth plays a role, as does everyone else; but she can be extremely direct when others trespass upon her dignity, as Lady Catherine and Darcy learn to their pain. She can also be guided by a benevolent impulse, whatever others may think, as when she walks three miles through mud to visit Jane. Elizabeth is at once a highly individual and a deeply social being, and her manners reflect this synthesis.

Jane Austen clearly appreciates the values of civilization; but she is aware, too, of the pitfalls and limitations of the established order. The code of civility regulates our impulses, provides patterns of interaction, and permits us to come together without continually hurting each other's feelings. At the same time, however, it inhibits self-expression, isolates us from each other, and makes knowledge and communication difficult. It is one of the major blocking forces in the comic action of the novel. Elizabeth and Darcy come together only after there have been major breakdowns of civility.

Skilled as they are in communicating their own feelings and interpreting those of others, the members of this society still make numerous mistakes. The masking effect of social forms combines with personal factors in both the actor and the observer to produce a wide range of misunderstandings. At the time of his first proposal, Darcy believes Elizabeth " 'to be wishing, expecting [his] addresses' " (III, xvi). Darcy's arrogance is partly responsible for this gross error, but he has also been misled by Elizabeth, who expresses her dislike under the guise of raillery. " 'My manners,' " says Elizabeth, " 'must have been at fault, but not intentionally I assure you.' " The reader, who is much better informed than he could be in real life, enjoys the irony not only of Darcy's, but also of Elizabeth's mistakes. In almost every exchange between them in the first half of the novel Darcy and Elizabeth misinterpret each other. He fails to understand her hostile and she his attentive behavior. An equally important failure of communication occurs, of course, between Jane and Bingley. Her manners are so generally agreeable and he is so diffident that Bingley fails to perceive how much he is loved. Their difficulties illustrate a recurring problem in Jane Austen: given the restrictive patterns of courtship and the modest behavior prescribed for women, how are young people to come to an understanding?

Since so much social behavior is a form of acting, it is difficult not only to express and interpret feelings, but also to read character. Miss Bingley is well understood by an astute observer like Elizabeth, but for a long time she deceives Jane. Even Elizabeth, however, is seriously mistaken about Wickham and Darcy. Wickham is a marvelous actor who charms everyone on first acquaintance. Darcy refuses to pretend (" 'disguise of every sort is my abhorrence' "—II, xi); and, as a result, he is highly unpopular. Wickham's "countenance, voice, and manner [establish] him at once in the possession of every virtue" (II, xiii); there is "truth in his looks." Darcy's manner disposes

Elizabeth not only to dislike him, but to beli...
gross misconduct.

Elizabeth's mistakes are cleared up and c...
with Darcy is established by the breakdown of t...
occurs when Darcy proposes. By dwelling upon h...
Elizabeth's "inferiority—of its being a degradation...
provokes her into a direct revelation of her feeling
charges concerning his mistreatment of Wickham an...
interference with Jane and Bingley set in motion the chain of
events, beginning with Darcy's letter, which eventually removes
most of the obstacles to the happy ending. The most serious
charge which Elizabeth makes, from Darcy's point of view, is
that he behaves in an ungentleman-like manner. This criticism
stings him to the core; he has always prided himself on being
well-bred.

By the time of Darcy's second proposal, both parties are
ashamed of their past conduct. Elizabeth accuses herself of
having " 'abused [him] so abominably to [his] face.' "

> "What did you say to me [replied Darcy], that I did not deserve.
> . . . my behavior to you at the time, had merited the severest reproof.
> It was unpardonable. I cannot think of it without abhorrence."
>
> "We will not quarrel for the greater share of blame annexed to that
> evening," said Elizabeth. "The conduct of neither, if strictly examined,
> will be irreproachable; but since then, we have both, I hope, improved
> in civility." (III, xvi)

What Elizabeth says is true; both were indecorous that evening,
though her conduct was provoked by his, and she is now being
gracious in accepting an equal share of the blame. The irony is
that if they had both remained civil, they would never have
come to know each other or themselves; and neither their
marriage nor that of Jane and Bingley would have taken place.

The final resolution is facilitated by two further violations
of decorum. When they meet at Pemberley, Darcy tries to show
through his manners that he has changed and that he is still
interested in Elizabeth; and Elizabeth tries to be responsive
without seeming forward. They separate, however, under adverse conditions (Lydia has run off with Wickham); and each is

doubt about the feelings of the other. The first breakthrough in communication occurs when Lydia reveals, in her characteristically reckless way, the secret of Darcy's presence at her marriage. Since the confidence has already been broken, Mrs. Gardiner can now disclose the full extent of Darcy's assistance to the family; and this encourages Elizabeth to believe that he may still love her. The second violation of decorum is Lady Catherine's attempt to coerce Elizabeth into promising that she will never marry her nephew. Here, as in the first proposal scene, Elizabeth is extremely outspoken. Lady Catherine's report of this conversation, which is intended to discourage Darcy's interest, has the opposite effect and leads to the second proposal: " 'It taught me to hope . . . as I had scarcely ever allowed myself to hope before. I knew enough of your disposition to be certain, that, had you been absolutely, irrevocably decided against me, you would have acknowledged it to Lady Catherine, frankly and openly' " (III, xvi). Elizabeth's earlier frankness, which Darcy had felt to be uncivil, now gives him confidence in his interpretation of her behavior.

4

Pride and Prejudice contains one highly developed mimetic character, Elizabeth Bennet, and a number of other characters who have clearly identifiable psychological traits and may be described as mimetic types. Darcy and Lady Catherine are clearly expansive, Bingley and Jane are self-effacing, and Charlotte and Mr. Bennet are detached. These characters cannot be analyzed in great detail, but they are interesting in their own right, apart from their aesthetic and thematic roles; and they are important people in the life of the heroine, whose own character is revealed in part by her attitudes toward and relations with them. I shall preface my study of Elizabeth, therefore, with a brief look at Jane, Bingley, Charlotte, and Mr. Bennet. I shall take up Darcy after analyzing Elizabeth.

Jane's most remarkable trait, of course, one which makes her a kind of humors character, is her tendency to think well of everybody.

"Oh! you are a great deal too apt you know [observes Elizabeth], to like people in general. You never see a fault in any body. . . . I never heard you speak ill of a human being in my life."

"I would wish not to be hasty in censuring any one; but I always speak what I think."

"I know you do; and it is *that* which makes the wonder. With your good sense, to be so honestly blind to the follies and nonsense of others! . . . to take the good of every body's character and make it still better, and say nothing of the bad—belongs to you alone." (I, iv)

Jane is insecure about her own worth and acceptability and needs to approve of everyone lest they disapprove of her. She defends herself against fears of rejection by being mild, affable, and unthreatening. If she likes others, they will like her. Her taboo is so powerful that she represses not only the expression, but even the awareness of negative attitudes. To maintain her picture of the world, she denies, rationalizes, and distorts. In the Darcy-Wickham affair, she tries hard to construct a version of the situation in which no one is to blame. She defends Charlotte's decision to marry Collins and exonerates Bingley in his abandonment of her, minimizing her own suffering so as not to accuse him.

Jane has a strong taboo not only against being critical, but also against being proud, especially of her own "goodness." Her gallant response to Bingley's desertion, which she interprets as "an error of fancy" on her side, evokes a paean of praise from Elizabeth: " 'My dear Jane . . . you are too good. Your sweetness and disinterestedness are really quite angelic; I do not know what to say to you. I feel as if I had never done you justice, or loved you as you deserve' " (II,i). This praise makes Jane anxious, and she restores her humility by "eagerly disclaim[ing] all extraordinary merit, and [throwing] back the praise on her sister's warm affection." In her version of things, it is not she who is good, but Elizabeth, whose affectionate nature leads her to say so. One of the reasons for Jane's admiration of Bingley is "his diffidence, and the little value he put[s] on his own goodness" (III, xiv).

Jane and Bingley are much alike, and it is natural for them to admire each other. Bingley's chief trait is his readiness to be led by others. When he says that if he should resolve to quit

Netherfield, he would probably be off in five minutes, Darcy observes that " 'if, as you were mounting your horse, a friend were to say, "Bingley, you had better stay till next week," you would probably do it, you would probably not go—and, at another word, might stay a month' " (I, x). A debate follows upon the merits of such behavior. The expansive Darcy, who is secretly proud of being " 'too little yielding . . . for the convenience of the world' " (I, xi), despises Bingley's deference to a mere request, while Elizabeth defends his susceptibility to " 'the influence of friendship and affection' " (I, x). She takes a different view of Bingley's compliance when it leads him to abandon Jane: "Much as she had always been disposed to like him, she could not think without anger, hardly without contempt, on that easiness of temper, that want of proper resolution which now made him the slave of his designing friends, and led him to sacrifice his own happiness to the caprice of their inclinations" (II, i).

Bingley's behavior is dictated by his diffidence, his lack of confidence in either his judgment or his worth. He gives up Jane because Darcy persuades him of her indifference: " 'He had before believed her to return his affection with sincere, if not with equal regard—But Bingley has great natural modesty, with a stronger dependence on my judgment than on his own.—To convince him, therefore, that he had deceived himself, was no very difficult point' " (II, xii). His insecurity makes it easy for him to believe that Jane does not love him (he had never believed her to have an "equal regard"), and his distrust of his own judgment makes him dependent on Darcy. In the end, Darcy leads him back to Jane as easily as he had steered him away: " 'His diffidence had prevented his depending on his own judgment in so anxious a case, but his reliance on mine, made every thing easy' " (III, xvi). Elizabeth "longed to observe that Mr. Bingley had been a most delightful friend; so easily guided that his worth was invaluable." Bingley and Darcy have a symbiotic relationship. Darcy enjoys exercising his power, while Bingley escapes the anxiety of having to make his own decisions and of taking responsibility for his life. It gives him a feeling of security to have his actions directed by Darcy.

Mr. Bennet, in his astute way, sums up the characters of Jane and Bingley and gives us a glimpse of some of the problems to which their weaknesses will expose them: " 'I have not a doubt of your doing very well together. Your tempers are by no means unlike. You are each so complying that nothing will ever be resolved on; so easy, that every servant will cheat you; and so generous, that you will always exceed your income' " (III, xiii). Our last distinct picture of Jane and Bingley is of their being imposed upon by Lydia and Wickham: "With the Bingleys they . . . frequently staid so long, that even Bingley's good humour was overcome, and he proceeded so far as to *talk* of giving them a hint to be gone" (III, xix).

When Elizabeth learns of Charlotte's decision to marry Mr. Collins, she finds it " 'unaccountable in every view' " (II, i). Jane, typically, takes a more generous position: " 'You do not make allowance enough for difference of situation and temper . . . . Remember that she is one of a large family; that as to fortune, it is a most eligible match; and be ready to believe, for every body's sake, that she may feel something like regard and esteem for our cousin.' " " 'My dear Jane,' " Elizabeth replies, " 'Mr. Collins is a conceited, pompous, narrow-minded, silly man; . . . and you must feel, as well as I do, that the woman who marries him cannot have a proper way of thinking.' " Jane, of course, is partly right; Charlotte's temper and situation are quite different from Elizabeth's. But Elizabeth is correct, too: there is something wrong with a sensitive and intelligent woman who is ready to marry Mr. Collins.

What Elizabeth cannot understand is Charlotte's resignation—the degree to which she has given up the hope of personal fulfillment through marriage. Charlotte wants to marry for the sake of security and status; but in view of her plainness, her lack of fortune, and her age, she does not expect to have much choice in the selection of a mate. She is determined to accept the first socially eligible offer, and she builds a variety of defenses to justify herself in advance and to reconcile herself to the prospect of personal frustration. She keeps her expectations very low; she does not think "highly either of men or of matrimony" (I, xxii). Marriage is "uncertain of giving happiness," but it is "the only honourable provision for well-educated women of small fortune and . . . their pleasantest preservative from want." She disguises her hopelessness as disenchanted realism, mature wisdom. Since most marriages turn out unhappily anyway, there is not much point in being particular. " 'Happiness in marriage,' " she tells Elizabeth,

> "is entirely a matter of chance. If the dispositions of the parties are ever so well known to each other, or ever so similar before-hand, it does not advance their felicity in the least. They always continue to grow sufficiently unlike afterwards to have their share of vexation; and it is better to know as little as possible of the defects of the person with whom you are to pass your life." (I, vi)

This is a transparent rationalization, as is her assertion to Elizabeth that her " 'chance of happiness' " with Collins " 'is as fair, as most people can boast on entering the marriage state' " (I, xxii).

The resigned attitude which leads Charlotte to marry Collins also makes it possible for her to live with him with far less pain than Elizabeth would experience in a like situation. She takes the same cold-blooded and practical attitude toward keeping Collins at a distance that she had taken earlier in encouraging his advances. During her visit to Hunsford, Elizabeth is compelled to appreciate Charlotte's "address in guiding, and composure in bearing with her husband, and to acknowledge that it was done very well" (II, v). We are left with the feeling, however, that Charlotte has committed herself to a barren existence by which she is bound, eventually, to feel oppressed. As the daughter of Sir William Lucas, Charlotte has had some experience in living with a hollow man; but we cannot help wondering if she will be forced, in time, to adopt the defensive irony of a Mr. Bennet.

Mr. Bennet is the most fully developed detached character that we have encountered so far in Jane Austen. Like Charlotte, he maintains his independence of an adverse fate by cultivating a philosophic resignation. He tries to confine his wants to what he can have and to develop a "don't care" attitude toward the sources of frustration. He retires into his library, as Charlotte does into her carefully positioned sitting room, and tries as much as possible to forget his family, as Charlotte endeavors to forget Collins. He busies himself with private pleasures and pursuits; and he is concerned with financial independence, not so much that he endeavors to save, but enough that, despite a spendthrift wife, he stays out of debt.

Mr. Bennet displays the desire for freedom which is typical of the detached person. This takes the form of a craving for serenity or peace, which "means for him simply the absence of all troubles, irritations, and upsets" *(NHG,* p. 263). " 'We shall have no peace at Longbourn,' " he tells Elizabeth, " 'if Lydia does not go to Brighton. Let her go then' " (II, xviii). Mr. Bennet wants to be left alone, to have nothing expected of him, to be unencumbered by responsibilities. He has a profound aversion to effort. As a result, he is a poor father, as the affair of Lydia clearly indicates. Wickham might have imagined, speculates Elizabeth, from her father's "indolence and the little attention he has ever given to what was going forward in his family, that *he* would do as little, and think as little about it, as any father could do in such a matter" (III, v).

Mr. Bennet is deeply affected by his daughter's disgrace and is stirred, "in the first transports of [his] rage," into activity. But he soon returns "to all his former indolence" (III, viii). He remains a "most negligent and dilatory correspondent," though "at such a time" his family "had hoped for exertion" (III, vi). When Mr. Gardiner arrives in London, he readily turns the affair over to him and returns to Longbourn with "all the appearance of his usual philosophic composure." He feels much to blame, but he assures Elizabeth, with considerable self-knowledge, that the "impression . . . will pass away soon enough," as it does. He has to be pushed into replying promptly to the news of Lydia's impending marriage; and he finds it "a very welcome surprise" that the difficulties have been resolved "with such trifling exertion on his side": "for his chief wish at present, was to have as little trouble in the business as possible" (III, viii). He is even more pleased when he learns that it is Darcy, now Elizabeth's fiancé, who has supplied the money: " 'So much the better. It will save me a world of trouble and economy' " (III, xvii).

Mr. Bennet's withdrawal is, in part at least, a reaction to his unhappy marriage:

> Captivated by youth and beauty, and that appearance of good humour, which youth and beauty generally give, [he] had married a woman whose weak understanding and illiberal mind, had very early in their marriage put an end to all real affection for her. . . . and all his views of domestic happiness were overthrown. But Mr. Bennet was not of a disposition to seek comfort for the disappointment which his own imprudence had brought on, in any of those pleasures which too often console the unfortunate for their folly or their vice. He was fond of the country and of books; and from these tastes had arisen his principal enjoyments. To his wife he was very little otherwise indebted, than as her ignorance and folly had contributed to his amusement. This is not the sort of happiness which a man would in general wish to owe to his wife; but where other powers of entertainment are wanting, the true philosopher will derive benefit from such as are given. (II, xix)

The impression I receive from this passage is that Mr. Bennet is a basically detached person who, prompted by his need for sexual love, mistakes the character of his intended wife and entertains, for a while, dreams of domestic felicity. When he sees his mistake, he does not console himself by pursuing other women but withdraws permanently from human relationships, which have proved to be so disappointing, and immerses himself in the pleasures of an intellectual and retired life. He inures himself to the pain of his situation by not caring. He disentangles himself emotionally, looks on from a distance, and consoles himself by being amused.

Mr. Bennet's amusement is not only a philosophic consolation, a "benefit" which can be derived from an otherwise bad situation; it is also a release of aggression and a defense against painful feelings. At some level, Mr. Bennet is deeply embittered by the ignorance and folly of his wife. His treatment of her is sadistic, demeaning, and contemptuous. Under the guise of wit, he engages in a "continual breach of conjugal obligation and decorum" which exposes "his wife to the contempt of her own children" (II, xix). He uses his superior intelligence to torment his wife in ways which avoid the direct expression of feeling and preserve his tranquillity.

Mr. Bennet is disappointed not only in his wife, but in his human relations generally. His daughters are, most of them, silly, and his neighbors are fools. He defends himself against the frustration inherent in this situation by regarding life as a comic spectacle. " 'For what do we live,' " he asks Elizabeth, " 'but to make sport for our neighbors, and to laugh at them in our turn' " (III, xv). It is others who provide the sport, of course, and Mr. Bennet who does the laughing. Everything that would pain him, if he were to take it seriously, he turns into a source of amusement. The "wild giddiness of his youngest daughters" (II, xiv), the foolishness of Collins (who is, after all, his heir apparent), and the sleaziness of Wickham, the first of his sons-in-law, all become transformed by his defensive detachment into jolly good jokes. This not only leads to irresponsibility, but also, at times, to a callous lack of human sympathy and concern. He is "gratified . . . to discover that Charlotte Lucas . . . [is] as foolish as his wife, and more foolish than his daughter" (I, xxiii). He seems to have no empathy whatever with Jane in her distress over Bingley:

> "So Lizzy," said he one day, "your sister is crossed in love I find. I congratulate her. Next to being married, a girl likes to be crossed in love a little now and then. . . . When is your turn to come? You will hardly bear to be long outdone by Jane. . . . Let Wickham be *your* man. He is a pleasant fellow, and would jilt you creditably." (II, i)

He would not be amused, however, if Elizabeth were actually to be hurt; for she is the one person he really cares about. He admires her intelligence and finds her to be a kindred spirit. She shares his satirical perspective and appreciates his wit. He listens to Collins "with the keenest enjoyment, . . . and except for an occasional glance at Elizabeth, requiring no partner in his pleasure" (I, xiv). Elizabeth's presence adds considerably to his enjoyment. Many of his sallies and satirical games are performances for which she is the audience. She provides him with something precious, another person who recognizes his talents and shares his attitude of amused contempt toward his fellows. She is the most important person in his life. He dislikes her leaving to visit Charlotte and says "more than once" upon her return, " 'I am glad you are come back, Lizzy' " (II, xvi). For Mr. Bennet, this is an extraordinary display of feeling. When he thinks that she wants to marry Darcy for purely social reasons, he abandons his detachment, pleads with her to reconsider, and reveals the extent of his own unhappiness:

> "But let me advise you to think better of it. I know your disposition, Lizzy, I know that you could be neither happy nor respectable, unless you truly esteemed your husband. . . . My child, let me not have the grief of seeing *you* unable to respect your partner in life. You know not what you are about." (III, xvii)

5

If asked to name the most attractive heroine in nineteenth century fiction, and the sanest, a great many readers would probably nominate Elizabeth Bennet. I would do so myself. For a long time I felt that Elizabeth was not a suitable subject for psychological analysis. It is customary to see her primarily as an aesthetic and an illustrative character; and her problems are considerably less severe (and hence less evident) than are those of Fanny and Emma. Her wit, charm, vitality, and intelligence also tend to obscure her defensive strategies. By calling attention to these strategies I shall obscure, I fear, the many positive aspects of her personality. This is not my intention, but it is one of the unavoidable dangers of psychological analysis. It does not do justice to a whole range of human qualities which make people with similar defenses very different from each other and quite variable in their attractiveness and humanity. Let me caution the reader, then, not to mistake Elizabeth's defenses for the whole of her being. My object, moreover, is not to prove that she has psychological problems but to gain a fuller understanding of why she acts and feels as she does. When we understand Elizabeth as a person, a creation inside a creation, we shall have reason once again to marvel at Jane Austen's psychological intuition and to admire her genius in characterization.

Elizabeth suffers, as do all of the Bennet girls, from the unhappy marriage of her parents, from their personal defects, and from their failure to provide a well-ordered and respectable family life. Mrs. Bennet supplies little in the way of mothering and offers no model of mature womanliness. Elizabeth grows

118

up wanting to be as unlike her mother as possible. She suffers not only from her mother's deficiencies, but also from her lack of affection; Elizabeth is "the least dear" of all her children (I, xviii). Elizabeth defends herself against the pain of having such a mother, and such a family, by detaching herself and being amused by what would otherwise hurt or embarrass her. She holds herself inwardly aloof and refuses to identify with most of her family.

Elizabeth is, in many respects, her father's daughter. She appreciates his abilities, adopts his defenses, and is grateful for his approval. Like him, she is a " 'studier of character' " (I, ix) who prides herself on her self-knowledge and her ability to see through others. She "love[s] absurdities" (II, xix): " 'Follies and nonsense, whims and inconsistencies do divert me, I own, and I laugh at them whenever I can' " (I, xi). She is able to remain detached even in rather difficult situations. When Mr. Collins proposes, she tries "to conceal by incessant employment the feelings which were divided between distress and diver-sion"(I, xix).

She is considerably less detached, however, than her father. Being younger and less frustrated than he, she is more hopeful, more idealistic, and more concerned about life generally. Being essentially undefeated (as opposed to her father, who has given up), Elizabeth takes herself, her values, and a chosen few of her relationships quite seriously. This makes her vulnerable in ways in which her father is not. She is deeply disturbed by Bingley's abandonment of Jane and by Charlotte's acceptance of Collins. There quickly emerges the dark view of the world against which her detachment has been a defense:

> There are few people whom I really love, and still fewer of whom I think well. The more I see of the world, the more am I dissatisfied with it; and every day confirms my belief of the inconsistency of all human characters, and of the little dependence that can be placed on the appearance of either merit or sense. (II, i)

Her reaction to Charlotte's behavior is especially intense. Apart from her father, Charlotte is the person in her world who is closest to her in temperament and intelligence. Isolated as she is, Elizabeth values the relationship greatly. She imagines Charlotte to be more like herself than she really is. When Charlotte expresses her cynical attitude toward the importance of selectivity in choosing a mate, Elizabeth cannot believe that she is serious: " 'You make me laugh, Charlotte; but it is not sound. You know it is not sound, and that you would never act in this way yourself' " (I, vi). When Charlotte does behave in this way, Elizabeth's belief in human nature, already guarded, is badly shaken. Her estimate of her own judgment, moreover, receives a blow—the first of several. She defends herself against future disappointments by lowering her expectations of people still farther and by turning "with fonder regard" to Jane, "of whose rectitude and delicacy she was sure her opinion would never be shaken" (I, xxiii). She dissociates herself from Charlotte and withdraws to a safer distance.

Elizabeth's pain in this situation is the result partly of hurt pride, partly of a sense of loss, and partly of her feeling of identification with Charlotte. She is threatened by Charlotte's fate, which violates her sense of personal dignity and shows a person like herself betraying herself and being trapped by life. Elizabeth needs to criticize her friend severely in order to reaffirm her own values and expectations.

When we compare Elizabeth with her father and her friend, we can see that, while she shares many of their characteristics, she is not basically detached. They have no hopes of mastering life and have resigned themselves to a reduced lot. Elizabeth, however, is expansive. She thinks well of herself, has high expectations, and will not settle for a position which is beneath her sense of her own deserts. Her expansiveness, like her detachment, derives in large measure from her father. He looks down upon almost everyone else, but Elizabeth is clearly his favorite and the object of his admiration. This recognition from the most important person in her world, a man whose abilities even Mr. Darcy must respect, feeds her pride and helps to compensate for her shame at her family and lack of approval from her mother. Her elevated conception of herself is reinforced by her superior abilities and the absence of any real competition in her family or social circles. Like her father, she finds that one of the compensations of living among fools is the pleasure of despising them. When she decides not to reveal what she has learned about Wickham, she observes to Jane that " 'sometime hence it will be all found out, and then we may laugh at their stupidity for not knowing it before' " (II, xviii).

Elizabeth's aggressiveness is most clearly visible when her pride is being threatened. She has a fear of being looked down upon and a need to show others that she cannot be laughed at, manipulated, or treated with condescension. In the defense of her pride, she becomes saucy, combative, and, sometimes, brutally frank. Some of this behavior seems like healthy self-assertion, as when she defies Lady Catherine near the end; but much of it is clearly defensive. When she first visits Lady Catherine at Rosings, she seems determined not to be overawed. As they ascend "the steps to the hall, Maria's alarm [is] every moment increasing, and even Sir William [does] not look perfectly calm," but "Elizabeth's courage [does] not fail her" (II, vi). The suggestion is that she is afraid that it would. Once inside, Sir William is "so completely awed, by the grandeur surrounding him, that he [has] but just courage enough to make a very low bow"; and Maria is "frightened almost out of her senses"; but Elizabeth finds "herself quite equal to the scene, and [can] observe the three ladies before her composedly." One senses that Elizabeth has steeled herself to this situation so as to maintain her sense of equality with Lady Catherine and superiority to Sir William Lucas. Her composure is a form of triumph. When she discovers that Lady Catherine is a fool, she becomes completely at her ease and even toys with her adversary by refusing immediately to disclose her age. Lady Catherine is not only a great lady, of course, but also a very manipulative one; and Elizabeth's satisfaction in trifling with her is evident.

We are now in a position to understand Elizabeth's reactions to Darcy. When Bingley urges Darcy to seek an introduction to Elizabeth, Darcy looks at her for a moment and then coldly replies, " 'She is tolerable; but not handsome enough to tempt *me;* and I am in no humour at present to give consequence to young ladies who are slighted by other men' " (I, iii). Elizabeth overhears this remark and is deeply offended. Being an expansive person herself, she can forgive Darcy's pride, which, as Charlotte observes, has some justification:

"One cannot wonder that so very fine a young man, with family, fortune, every thing in his favour, should think highly of himself. If I may so express it, he has a *right* to be proud."

"That is very true," replied Elizabeth, "and I could easily forgive *his* pride, if he had not mortified *mine.*" (I, iii)

Elizabeth is mortified partly because of the nature of her claims and partly because she has been rejected by a man of such importance, a man of her own type whom she cannot easily dismiss. She is accustomed to think highly of *herself,* and one might guess that she had been hoping for some form of recognition from the Netherfield party. Instead Darcy places himself well above her and interprets her not dancing as a sign of her unattractiveness to other men.

For someone like Elizabeth, this is a severe blow; and she works hard from this point on to soften the pain, to restore her pride, and to protect herself against further injury. Her immediate reaction is to make a joke of what has happened: "She told the story . . . with great spirit among her friends; for she had a lively, playful disposition, which delighted in anything ridiculous" (I, iii). The implied author's analysis is rather misleading here. Elizabeth's telling the story is not the manifestation of a lively disposition. It is a defensive technique which serves several purposes. It distances her from her hurt feelings, it denies the significance of the event by turning it into an object of laughter, and it gains an immediate revenge on Darcy by making him ridiculous in the eyes of others. Jane Austen at once creates and is taken in by Elizabeth's facade.

In almost every encounter that she has with Darcy between the initial insult and the receipt of his letter Elizabeth is highly defensive; and, as a result, she misperceives him constantly. As he becomes more and more attracted to her, she continues to assume his ill will; and she interprets his various displays of interest as forms of aggression. In order to know more of her, he listens to her conversation with Colonel Forster. Elizabeth is afraid that he is observing her in order to find grounds for ridicule: " 'He has a very satirical eye, and if I do not begin by being impertinent myself, I shall soon grow afraid of him' " (I, vi). She is projecting her own attitudes onto Darcy; and she fears that he is regarding her as she regards those to whom she feels superior.

While she is at Netherfield, caring for Jane, Elizabeth cannot help noticing how frequently Darcy's eyes are fixed upon her.

> She hardly knew how to suppose that she could be an object of admiration to so great a man; and yet that he should look at her because he disliked her, was still more strange. She could only imagine however at last, that she drew his notice because there was something about her more wrong and reprehensible, according to his ideas of right, than in any other person present. The supposition did not pain her. She liked him too little to care for his approbation. (I, x)

She will not allow herself to suppose that she might be an object of Darcy's admiration because to do so would make her vulnerable if she should be wrong. Darcy has hurt her once, badly; and she is going to make sure that it does not happen again. It is much safer to suppose that he is antagonistic and to attribute this to his arrogance and snobbish values. She fortifies herself against his presumed criticism by holding onto a fixed dislike. She disapproves of him so much that his attitude toward her is of no importance.

When Miss Bingley plays a lively Scotch air and Darcy asks her to dance, Elizabeth's response is highly defensive.

> She smiled, but made no answer. He repeated the question, with some surprise at her silence.
> "Oh!" said she, "I heard you before, but I could not immediately determine what to say in reply. You wanted me, I know, to say 'Yes,' that you might have the pleasure of despising my taste; but I always delight in overthrowing those kind of schemes, and cheating a person of their premeditated contempt. I have therefore made up my mind to tell you, that I do not want to dance a reel at all—and now despise me if you dare."
> "Indeed I do not dare." (I, x)

Elizabeth makes no answer at first because she cannot analyze immediately the motive behind Darcy's invitation, but she is certain that it is insulting and that he is setting a trap. She is especially sensitive on the subject of dancing since Darcy's refusal to dance with her was the initial offense. When, during a gathering at Longbourn, Sir William Lucas had attempted to pair them off in a dance, Darcy was not unwilling, but Elizabeth drew back immediately. One way to avoid being injured again by Darcy is to reject him as a partner before he has a chance to reject her. This shows him that his initial slight does not matter, since she does not want to dance with him anyway; and it has the additional satisfaction of being a retaliation, of doing to him what he has done to her.

Elizabeth's manner in the Netherfield episode is a mixture of "sweetness and archness" (I, x). She has enough control of her feelings to conceal her sense of being threatened (any revelation of which would be a defeat) and to express her defensiveness in the form of raillery. Knowing her own feelings and having a distorted picture of Darcy, she expects Darcy to be affronted. But the disguise of wit, combined with Darcy's enjoyment of her aggressiveness, produces the opposite effect, and he is charmed.

Elizabeth misperceives Darcy again at Rosings when he stations himself near the piano "so as to command a full view of the fair performer's countenance" (II, viii):

> "You mean to frighten me, Mr. Darcy, by coming in all this state to hear me? But I will not be alarmed though your sister *does* play so well. There is a stubbornness about me that never can bear to be frightened at the will of others. My courage always rises with every attempt to intimidate me."

Elizabeth *is* alarmed, of course. She is insecure about her own playing, and she fears Darcy's judgment. Her aggressiveness is designed to assure herself that she is living up to her expansive shoulds ("I should not be afraid of anyone") and to show Darcy that he has no power over her. Her reactions are so entirely inappropriate that Darcy cannot take them seriously: " 'I shall not say that you are mistaken,' he replied, 'because you could not really believe me to entertain any design of alarming you.' "

Elizabeth's receptiveness to Wickham's slanders is yet another manifestation of her defensiveness. Darcy is one of the few people in her experience to whom she has not been able to feel easily superior. This is why his insulting behavior rankles her so. Had she been less deeply hurt, she might have been able to observe his interest and attraction. As it is, she interprets his behavior as consistently threatening and defends her pride by finding him haughty and disagreeable. She is comforted by the fact that " 'he is not at all liked in Hertfordshire,' " that " 'every body is disgusted with his pride' " (I, xvi). She has a need to tear him down, to think the worst. The more deficient he is, the less weight she must give to his judgment of her. She is at once outraged and gratified by Wickham's account of his behavior: " 'This is quite shocking!—He deserves to be publicly disgraced' " (I, xvi). She can express on Wickham's behalf all of the anger which she has been feeling toward Darcy on her own account. Wickham's tale justifies her judgment and shows Darcy to be even worse than she had thought. She is now clearly superior to the man whose rejection has pained her so much.

Her receptiveness has something to do also with her feelings toward Wickham. Had her critical faculties been awake, she would have noted the impropriety of his disclosures; and she might have been less credulous. But she is blinded, as she herself comes to see, by the gratification of her pride which his attentions afford. Wickham is an attractive man, a general favorite, and therefore a prize. Unlike Darcy, he singles Elizabeth out immediately for special attention and makes her his confidant. He is not a suitable match, and Elizabeth is no more in love with him than Emma is in love with Frank Churchill; but, like Emma, she wishes to make a conquest. She dresses for the Netherfield ball with "more than usual care, and prepare[s] in the highest spirits for the conquest of all that remained unsubdued of his heart" (I, xviii). She receives Mrs. Gardiner's cautions rationally, however, because she does not really want to make a disadvantageous marriage; and she is content when Wickham shifts his attentions to Miss King: "Her heart had been but slightly touched, and her vanity was satisfied with believing that *she* would have been his only choice, had fortune permitted it" (II, iii). Wickham gives Elizabeth the recognition, the affirmation of special worth, for which she hungers and which Darcy had denied. Her strong prepossession against the one and in favor of the other, from the very beginning of their acquaintance, suggests her vulnerability and the strength of her needs.

Elizabeth's anger toward Darcy is fed by her discovery of his role in separating Jane and Bingley, and it is released by his insulting behavior during his proposal. Darcy once again injures her pride. He admires her personally, but he is deeply troubled by her family connections; and he speaks, rather compulsively, "of his sense of her inferiority . . . of the family obstacles which judgment had always opposed to inclination" (II, xi). Elizabeth is especially vulnerable on this point. She has been herself deeply ashamed of her family, and she has defended herself by detachment and a sense of superiority. What Darcy is saying is that her family's inferiority is also her own, and that because of her connections, she is beneath him. By letting him know that she has " 'never desired [his] good opinion,' " she nullifies his objections and restores her pride. It is he, not she, who is undesirable.

When Darcy wishes to know " 'why, with so little *endeavour* at civility, [he] is thus rejected,' " Elizabeth defends her behavior by attacking his violation of decorum in expressing his reservations. She proceeds to levy her complaints on behalf of Jane and of Wickham, both of whom, as she sees it, have had their happiness destroyed by Darcy. Darcy is disturbed by her low opinion of him; but, since he feels that it is undeserved, he reacts not by meeting her charges, but by defending his " 'honest confession of . . . scruples,' " which he feels less comfortable about, and which he believes to be the basis of her rejection:

> "Disguise of every sort is my abhorrence. Nor am I ashamed of the feelings I related. They were natural and just. Could you expect me to rejoice in the inferiority of your connections? To congratulate myself on the hope of relations, whose condition in life is so decidedly beneath my own?"

This, of course, repeats the offense, and Elizabeth feels "herself growing more angry every moment." She retaliates in a devastating way by recounting the history of her dislike and affirming her " 'fullest belief in [his] arrogance, [his] conceit, and [his] selfish disdain of the feelings of others.' " Darcy replies with dignity, but he leaves hastily in a state of evident humiliation.

Painful as it is, the proposal scene is, on the whole, a great triumph for Elizabeth. Her pride is gratified in a variety of ways. She retaliates for all past and present injuries and has, at the same time, the immense satisfaction of having received an offer of marriage from the great Mr. Darcy. In the contest of personalities, it is decidedly she who is the winner. Darcy can say nothing for which she has not an overwhelming reply. He insults her by speaking of her family's inferiority; but she mortifies him by denouncing his character, attacking his manners and morals, and declaring that he is " 'the last man in the world whom [she] could ever be prevailed on to marry.' " Once he leaves, she is free to appreciate the significance of his proposal:

> That she should receive an offer of marriage from Mr. Darcy! that he should have been in love with her for so many months! so much in love as to wish to marry her in spite of all the objections which had made him prevent his friend's marrying her sister, and which must appear at least with equal force in his own case, was almost incredible! it was gratifying to have inspired unconsciously so strong an affection.

Given Elizabeth's craving for recognition, and her earlier feelings of rejection, this is a triumph indeed, one which she cannot help dwelling upon with great satisfaction. She can hardly wait till they arrive at the privacy of Longbourn in order to tell the story that "would so exceedingly astonish Jane, and must at the same time, so highly gratify whatever of her own vanity she had not yet been able to reason away" (II, xv).

In order to restore *his* pride, which has been deeply hurt, Darcy writes a letter in his own defense. Its contents are so threatening that Elizabeth reacts initially with anger and denial. Then her resistance collapses, and she is flooded with self-hate and depression. The significance of the letter from a psychological point of view is that it penetrates her defenses and makes it more difficult for her thereafter to maintain her feelings of superiority and detachment. The self-knowledge which she gains does not, of course, rid her of her faults, as the implied author would have us believe; but it does contribute to the changes in her defense system which prepare her for marriage to Darcy.

Elizabeth's self-hate arises largely from the discovery of her errors, which are particularly humiliating to someone who prides herself, as she does, upon her superior penetration. She is also disturbed by her recognition of the justice of Darcy's objections to her family: " 'The situation of your mother's family, though objectionable, was nothing in comparison of that total want of propriety so frequently, so almost uniformly betrayed by herself, by your three younger sisters, and occasionally even by your father' " (II, xii). When she first reads this passage, she is "too angry to have any wish of doing him justice"; but when she returns to it later, "her sense of shame [is] severe." When she realizes "how materially the credit of both [herself and Jane] must be hurt by such impropriety of conduct, she [feels] depressed beyond anything she had ever known" (II, xiii).

Elizabeth is so depressed because her detachment from her family has been broken down, and she is being forced to feel the painfulness of her situation. What has happened to Jane may well happen to her; and, in any event, she seems fated to share in the discredit which her family brings upon itself. She begins to dwell, as never before, upon the seriousness of her plight and upon the deficiencies of her father. She has "never been blind" to her father's failings, "but respecting his abilities, and grateful for his affectionate treatment of herself, she [has] endeavored to forget what she could not overlook, and to banish from her thoughts [his continual] breach of conjugal obligation and decorum." Elizabeth has repressed her criticism partly because she has tried to detach herself generally from the family's problems, and partly because her father's support has been so important to her. She could not afford to be in conflict with him or to have his status, and therefore the value of his praise, diminished in her own eyes. Her critical attitudes emerge now because she feels personally threatened by his irresponsibility. Her criticism of him constitutes, however, an additional blow to her pride.

Elizabeth's depression has another important source which we have not yet examined. It is the response of an expansive person who wishes to control his own fate to feelings of helplessness. She has always felt that her value was independent of her connections and has insisted upon being treated in accordance with her own high self-estimate. She sees now, however, that her image in the eyes of others is not something which she can completely determine and that she will always be saddled with her family's shame. She feels trapped in a situation which she is powerless to change. The "unhappy defects of her family" are "hopeless of remedy. Her father, contented with laughing at them, would never exert himself to restrain the wild giddiness of his youngest daughters; and her mother, with manners so far from right herself, was entirely insensible of the evil" (II, xiv). In the face of this, there is little that she and Jane can do.

Elizabeth is deeply depressed for only a short time. Her defenses are shaken, but they are by no means shattered. She has at her command, moreover, various pride-restoring devices. She is humbled by her discoveries about herself, but proud of her self-knowledge. The thought of Darcy's offer is a great consolation, and she amuses herself the next morning by wondering what Lady Catherine's reactions would have been had she accepted. She tells Jane that her behavior toward Darcy has been " 'very weak and vain and nonsensical' " (II, xvii); but a few moments later she is her arrogant self once more, as she looks forward to laughing at everyone's stupidity when the truth about Wickham is known. She can no longer be detached about her family. She tries to be "diverted" by the Brighton affair, "but all sense of pleasure [is] lost in shame" (II, xviii). She handles her discomfort by trying to do something about it, despite her feeling that nothing will ever change. She points out to her father " 'the very great disadvantages to us all, which must arise from the public notice of Lydia's unguarded and imprudent manner,' " and urges him to exercise his authority. But Mr. Bennet refuses; and Elizabeth, though she is "disappointed and sorry," suffers no return of her own earlier despair. She consoles herself with a sense of her own rectitude and derives some satisfaction, no doubt, from being more perceptive than her father.

By the time she leaves on her trip with the Gardiners, Elizabeth is outwardly as buoyant as ever. But inwardly, she has been somewhat subdued. As a result of her errors and of her stronger identification with her family, she no longer thinks quite so highly of herself or of her claims upon the world. Her need for recognition and preeminence is unabated, however.

Indeed, it is intensified by frustration, by the diminution of her self-esteem and of the value of her father's admiration. Her pride is suffering. This makes her extremely receptive to Pemberley and to the renewed attentions of Darcy.

Darcy's letter clears away many of Elizabeth's objections to his character. It does not arouse, however, a desire for his attentions or regret for her decision. Within an hour of her first sight of Pemberley, however, Elizabeth does experience "something like regret" (III, i). When Jane asks her later how long she has loved Darcy, Elizabeth replies, " 'I believe I must date it from my first seeing his beautiful grounds at Pemberley' " (III, xvii). Jane dismisses this as a joke (with the seeming concurrence of the implied author), and most critics have done likewise. But things said in jest often reveal the deepest truths; and our understanding of Elizabeth's character gives us good reason to take her answer seriously.

The magnificence of Pemberley not only wins Elizabeth's admiration, it also feeds her pride: "She had never seen a place for which nature had done more, or where natural beauty had been so little counteracted by an awkward taste. . . . and at that moment she felt, that to be mistress of Pemberley might be something!" (III, i). It may or may not be the case that the grounds of Pemberley are intended as a reflection of Darcy the man—he has only been in possession, after all, for five years; but it is most certainly true that their beauty and the grandeur of the house bring home to Elizabeth the magnitude of Darcy's proposal and the elevation which it might have bestowed upon her. She has never seen a more beautiful place, and the admiration of the Gardiners feeds her sense of triumph. Her reactions to the furnishings bring out more clearly the competitive element in her response. She not only admires Darcy's taste, but she also compares Pemberley with Rosings and triumphs thereby over Lady Catherine. She is caught up for a moment or two in a fantasy of possession:

> "And of this place," thought she, "I might have been mistress! With these rooms I might now have been familiarly acquainted! Instead of viewing them as a stranger, I might have rejoiced in them as my own, and welcomed to them as visitors my uncle and aunt."

The thought that she would not have been allowed to invite the Gardiners is "a lucky recollection—it save[s] her from something like regret." Her imagined joy in the rooms is not so much pleasure in their beauty as glory in their possession. The fantasy of welcoming her uncle and aunt is also one of personal grandeur. Being mistress of Pemberley would be like having a dream come true. Her desires for power, recognition, and ascendancy would be gratified beyond all reasonable expectation.

If, before, Elizabeth was disposed to think ill of Darcy because he had hurt her pride, she is now disposed to think well of him because he has fed it. The more admirable he is, the more gratifying is his proposal and the greater is its tribute to herself. She defends herself against regret by remembering Darcy's haughtiness, but she is extraordinarily receptive to Mrs. Reynolds' praise of him and is as ready now to credit an account in his favor as she had been before to believe Wickham's slanders. When Mrs. Reynolds speaks of Darcy's good temper, "her keenest attention" is awakened and she longs "to hear more." When she praises his affability to the poor, Elizabeth "listen[s], wonder[s], doubt[s], and [is] impatient for more." " 'He is the best landlord, and the best master,' " declares Mrs. Reynolds, " 'that ever lived.' "

As Elizabeth contemplates his portrait, her changed feelings toward Darcy begin to crystallize:

> The commendation bestowed on him by Mrs. Reynolds was of no trifling nature. What praise is more valuable than the praise of an intelligent servant? As a brother, a landlord, a master, she considered how many people's happiness were in his guardianship!—How much of pleasure or pain it was in his power to bestow!—How much of good or evil must be done by him! . . . as she stood before the canvas, on which he was represented, and fixed his eyes upon herself, she thought of his regard with a deeper sentiment of gratitude than it had ever raised before; she remembered its warmth, and softened its impropriety of expression. (III, i)

Elizabeth dwells here not only on Darcy's goodness, his sense of responsibility, but also upon his power, upon the number of people who are dependent upon him. Her deeper sentiment of gratitude derives from her more vivid perception of his greatness as well as from her new appreciation of his character. Her gratitude springs to a large extent from gratified pride. It is appreciation for having been loved by so great a man, for having been done such an honor.

Since Darcy's exaltation is now her own, Elizabeth has a vested interest in believing the best of him and in suppressing awareness of his faults. Mrs. Reynolds' testimony is valid as far as Darcy's relation to his dependents is concerned, but this does not change the fact that he is stiff and haughty with members of his own social class who are strangers or whom he believes to be beneath him in wealth or status. As Colonel Fitzwilliam observed, he is a man who likes to have his own way and who is ill qualified to recommend himself to strangers " 'because he will not give himself the trouble' " (II, viii). According to Darcy's own account, he was " 'spoilt' " by his parents, who " 'allowed, encouraged, almost taught [him] to be selfish and overbearing, to care for none beyond [his] own family circle, to think meanly of the rest of the world' " (III, xvi). This seems to be an accurate self-characterization. Elizabeth was highly conscious of Darcy's " 'arrogance, . . . conceit, and . . . selfish disdain of the feelings of others' " (II, xi) when his pride was in conflict with her own. As she transfers her pride to him, she becomes increasingly blind to his faults, until she announces to her father, after the second proposal, that " 'he has no improper pride. He is perfectly amiable' " (III, xvii). She sees him in this way partly because he has been so courteous to her and to the Gardiners and partly because she cannot see as improper a pride which is identical with her own.

It is evident that as she stands before Darcy's portrait, Elizabeth is already disposed to want him in marriage. Within a few minutes of his appearance, she is actively hoping that he still loves her. The marriage of Elizabeth and Darcy is supposed to illustrate the balancing of social and personal values, but Elizabeth's change of feeling is produced almost entirely by Darcy's wealth and grandeur. It is facilitated by the clearing away of objections to his character; but it has little to do with such positive values as temperamental compatibility, mutuality of interests and attitudes, strong personal liking, or respect based upon intimate knowledge. Both the novelist and her heroine are at pains to justify Elizabeth's desire for Darcy in terms of consciously acceptable values and to obscure its real psychological basis. Jane Austen contrasts Elizabeth's regard for Darcy, which is based on "gratitude and esteem," with her partiality for Wickham, which was based upon love at first sight (III, iv); but the comparison is misleading and will not hold. Elizabeth is attracted to both men because they feed her pride. She wants Darcy because such a marriage would satisfy her expansive needs for glory, for competitive triumph, and for recognition of her worth. She wants him because to be mistress of Pemberley would be somthing!

Elizabeth is attracted to Darcy, also, of course, because she is immensely flattered by his continuing affection for her. When she first encounters him at Pemberley, she reacts in a typically defensive way: "She was overpowered by shame and vexation. Her coming there was the most unfortunate, the most ill-judged thing in the world! How strange it must appear to him! In what a disgraceful light might it not strike so vain a man! It might seem as if she had purposely thrown herself in his way again!" (III, ii). Elizabeth feels threatened once again by Darcy's pride. She is afraid of seeming to want him (which she does) while he no longer wants her. His gentleness and civility quiet her fears; and his attentions to the Gardiners, in whose refinement she glories, "gratif[y] her exceedingly; the compliment must be all for herself." She guesses immediately that he has changed because of her, but she is afraid to believe this lest her hopes rise too high and expose her to a humiliating disappointment. His invitation to meet his sister and his continued courtesy to the Gardiners are unmistakable signs of his interest, however; and Elizabeth becomes fairly confident of her "power" to bring on "the renewal of his addresses." Her desire to do so, which is growing steadily stronger, is motivated in large part by gratitude. "Such a change in a man of so much pride, excited not only astonishment but gratitude—for to love, ardent love, it must be attributed" (III, ii).

There is no indication that Elizabeth's feelings for Darcy ever approach a state of "ardent love." She regards him on his later visit to Longbourn "with an interest, if not quite so tender, at least as reasonable and just, as what Jane felt for Bingley"

(III, xi). Darcy, however, is "a man violently in love" (III, xvi); and Elizabeth, during her visit to Pemberley, is deeply moved by the tribute of his affection. She is fully alive now, as she had not been at Hunsford, to family obstacles and to the injustice of her accusations. Darcy's greatness and pride no longer make her feel inferior but rather fill her with a sense of triumph, for they have yielded to love for her—that is, to her value and attractiveness as a person. From Jane Austen's point of view, Elizabeth's gratitude is an admirable feminine emotion; but it comes, as I have said before, from the gratification of expansive claims, from gratified pride. Darcy endears himself to Elizabeth by saving her from the lowered self-esteem into which she had fallen and confirming her idealized image. This is a potent attraction. Now that she respects him, Darcy's love means that she *is,* after all, a superior being, an appropriate mate for "one of the most illustrious personages" in England (III, xv), a woman whose personal worth is so great as to compensate for the undesirability of her connections.

Elizabeth's hopes are dealt a severe blow by the arrival of Jane's letters announcing Lydia's elopement with Wickham: "Her power was sinking; everything *must* sink under such a proof of family weakness, such an assurance of the deepest disgrace" (III, iv). Darcy is not deterred, as we learn later; but this turn of events has an important impact upon Elizabeth's feelings, both toward herself and toward Darcy. It damages her pride further, making her need Darcy the more. It gives Darcy an opportunity to behave gallantly, thus enhancing her esteem for him. And it decreases her social prestige still farther, making Darcy's continued interest all the more evidence of his ardent love and her surpassing value.

The disgrace of her sister is a serious threat to Elizabeth's self-esteem. She reproaches herself severely for not having warned everyone of Wickham's character, she feels humiliated at the thought of the neighbors' triumph, and she is convinced that the family's taint must extend to herself and destroy her chances of marrying Darcy. Her self-effacing trends, which were most evident before in her admiration for Jane, emerge now rather powerfully. They result in self-abasement, irrational feelings of guilt, and the transfer of her pride to Darcy:

She was humbled, she was grieved; she repented, though she hardly knew of what. She became jealous of his esteem, when she could no longer hope to be benefited by it. . . . What a triumph for him, as she often thought, could he know that the proposals which she had proudly spurned only four months ago, would now have been gladly and gratefully received! . . . It was a union that must have been to the advantage of both; by her ease and liveliness, his mind might have been softened, his manner improved, and from his judgment, information, and knowledge of the world, she must have received benefit of greater importance. (III, viii)

Her repentance is a self-effacing response to misfortune; she must be somehow to blame. After having overestimated herself and undervalued Darcy, she swings now to the opposite pole. Her ease and liveliness can give something of value to him; but it is trivial compared with the benefits which his judgment and knowledge can bestow upon her. The crushing of her pride brings out her feelings of dependency. She gives up her struggle to assert her equality, recognizes how grateful she would be if Darcy would only ask her again, and experiences her pride in a self-effacing way by exalting him. She has a similar response when she hears of his role in promoting Lydia's marriage: "For herself she was humbled; but she was proud of him" (III, x).

The pattern of Elizabeth's development is familiar, of course, from our study of *Emma*. There are important differences, however. Elizabeth's humility and self-abasement reflect a relatively minor phase in her psychological evolution. She is suffering more from other people's faults than from her own; and, like Fanny Price, she is vindicated rather than chastened by the unfolding of the action. The events which threaten her pride have the final effect of reinforcing it. The elopement of her sister leads to a far greater triumph than she would have had before by leading Darcy to demonstrate her supreme importance to him. Once Elizabeth's pride is restored—indeed, inflated—by Darcy's second proposal, she is her expansive self again. After she marries, she revenges herself upon her mother by keeping her away; and she seems no less disposed than Darcy to maintain a clannish exclusivity. She is surrounded, as we have seen, by those who are respectful, deferential, or warmly appreciative of her merit. As we close the book, she is once again showing Darcy by her "lively and sportive manner" that she does not fear him and that she is, at least, his equal.

The thematic pattern of *Pride and Prejudice* is one in which the protagonists are both flawed by pride and are prejudiced as a result—Elizabeth toward Darcy and Darcy toward people of lower status who are outside of his immediate circle. Each has his pride chastened by the other and is awakened to realities about himself and others to which he has hitherto been blind. Elizabeth comes to question her superior perception, to recognize Darcy's merits, and to accept the implications of her social identity. Darcy, likewise, is " 'properly humbled' ":

> "I have been a selfish being all my life, in practice, though not in principle. . . . I was given good principles, but left to follow them in pride and conceit . . . Such I was, from eight to eight and twenty; and such I might still have been but for you, dearest, loveliest Elizabeth! What do I not owe to you! You taught me a lesson, hard indeed at first, but most advantageous. . . . You showed me how insufficient were all my pretensions to please a woman worthy of being pleased." (III, xvi)

His humiliation produces the self-insight which he displays in this passage, the remarkable change in manners which Elizabeth observes at Pemberley, and a transcendence of his former prejudices in his determination to ally himself with Elizabeth despite the increased undesirability of her family.

When we understand Elizabeth and Darcy as people, the implied author's interpretation is rather difficult to accept. They both achieve some genuine insight into themselves, but the experiences which they undergo are hardly enough to produce major changes in their personalities. If Darcy's description of himself is correct, being chastened by Elizabeth could not have purged him of all that "pride and conceit," though it is understandable that he should think so. Though he is less fully developed as a character, Darcy is, like Elizabeth, a creation inside a creation. His development is psychologically comprehensible, but it does not illustrate what it is supposed to. What happens between Darcy and Elizabeth is that they first hurt and then restore each other's pride. We have examined this pattern in Elizabeth. Darcy's development is not exactly parallel, but it is in many respects similar.

Darcy is an arrogant man who feels contempt for most of his fellows, as his opening remarks reveal. He enjoys manipulating compliant people like Bingley, but he despises them in his heart. He must wonder, like Mrs. Reynolds, when he will ever marry. Who is good enough for him? It would not feed his pride to connect himself with a sychophant like Miss Bingley. He needs a woman whom he can respect and whose appreciation of him will mean something. He is attracted to Elizabeth by her intelligence and her aggressiveness. Elizabeth's analysis is, as far as it goes, quite accurate. He admired her for her "impertinence": " 'The fact is, that you were sick of civility, of deference, of officious attention. You were disgusted with women who were always speaking and looking, and thinking for *your* approbation alone. I roused and interested you, because I was so unlike *them*' "(III, xviii). Elizabeth has pride; she is a challenge, another strong personality, a mental equal. It does not occur to Darcy, however, that he must win her. He assumes, in his conceit, that she would be overjoyed by an offer from *him*. His mental energy is taken up, rather, by his inner conflict, by the struggles which he describes to her in the course of his proposal. He *must* tell her about his reservations in order to assuage his feelings of humiliation. Describing his sense of degradation has the effect of restoring, in some measure at least, the pride which he is offending.

He reacts to Elizabeth's denunciations in several ways. His letter clears him of the charges concerning Jane and Wickham. What hurts him the most is her attack on his ungentlemanlike behavior and his "selfish disdain for the feelings of others" (II, xi). He is vulnerable to these criticisms for two reasons: (1) he cannot discredit their source, since he has allowed himself to feel respect for Elizabeth, and (2) he has prided himself on behaving in an exemplary manner, on being a true gentleman. He was given high standards by his parents, and he has identified himself with them. Until Elizabeth tells him otherwise, he has always felt himself to be living up to his shoulds. The collapse of this illusion damages his pride, and he is flooded with self-hate. The recollection of his behavior, he tells Elizabeth later, "is now, and has been many months, inexpressibly painful to me. Your reproof, so well applied, I shall never forget: 'had you behaved in a more gentleman-like manner.' Those were your words. You know not, you can scarcely conceive, how they have tortured me;—though it was some time, I confess, before I was reasonable enough to allow their justice." (III, xvi)

We may summarize Darcy's development in the following way. His parents provided him with both high standards and unqualified approval. As a result, he identifies himself with his idealized image in a narcissistic manner and feels very proud of himself. His pride is shaky, however, since it is not solidly founded on performance; and he develops a need to reinforce it by scorning others. This behavior is in conflict with his standards; but his defensive needs, combined with a continuous supply of praise and deference, keep him from being aware of the disparity between his principles and his practice. He places his pride at risk by allowing himself to admire Elizabeth so much that he would make a social sacrifice in order to gain her. This makes her opinion quite important to him. He assumes that she will both want and admire him, as everyone else always has. His narcissism and his perfectionism receive severe blows from Elizabeth's assault. He experiences intense self-hate, and as a defense he blames his parents and replaces them with Elizabeth as his primary moral guide.

As a result of Elizabeth's rejection, Darcy develops, for the first time in his life, a profound and agonizing dependency. What Elizabeth has told him, in effect, is that he is not his idealized, but rather his despised self: " 'You thought me then devoid of every proper feeling, I am sure you did' " (III, xvi). Elizabeth becomes the central figure in his psychic life. His overwhelming need is to repair his pride, and this can be done only through her. He must change his image in her eyes; he must win her approbation. His behavior at Pemberley and in the Lydia-Wickham affair is a direct reply to her charges. Only if she accepts him in marriage can he be completely vindicated and his self-esteem repaired. With Elizabeth's acceptance, Darcy's pride is restored, though he is less narcissistic than he was before. The major change in him is that he tries harder to live up to his principles and that he is dependent upon Elizabeth's approval for his sense of worth.

The marriage of Elizabeth and Darcy is offered as a model of "connubial felicity" (III, ix). As marriages in Jane Austen go, it is relatively attractive; but it is not as well founded as the implied author believes it to be. Elizabeth and Darcy are bound together by the complex interdependency of their pride systems. The marriage itself fulfills some important needs; it provides recognition and status for Elizabeth, vindication and approval for Darcy. But each remains wary of the other's susceptibilities and dependent on the other for the confirmation of his idealized image. Darcy's fear and dependency are greater than Elizabeth's, making him more overtly acquiescent; but Elizabeth is careful not to push him too far. His need to win her approval is matched by her need to think well of him, to share in his grandeur, and to repress her reservations. They are happy at the end because they have a vested interest in exalting each other. This makes for a rewarding, though, I should think, a somewhat tense relationship. They will get along well as long as each continues to feed the other's pride.

5

Persuasion

1

Persuasion is at once Jane Austen's most serious and her most romantic novel. For almost one-half of the novel the protagonist is in a seemingly hopeless situation. Anne Elliot is Austen's most completely deserving heroine, but she is being rewarded neither by fate nor by other people, and she faces the prospect of a blighted existence. She is far more passionately in love than Elinor, Elizabeth, Fanny or Emma; but she seems to have lost Wentworth forever and, along with him, the bloom of youth which could make her attractive to an equally desirable man. She is a melancholy figure, in mourning for her life, who can achieve at best a "desolate tranquillity."

All of this is changed, rapidly, indeed, almost miraculously, during the episode in Lyme. Jane Austen's love stories are always facilitated by a certain amount of authorial manipulation. In *Persuasion,* the manipulation is much more blatant than in the other novels. Having placed Anne in such a bleak situation, Austen extricates her by recourse to the conventions not only of comedy, but also of romance. From the Lyme episode onward a number of fortuitous circumstances occur which remove the obstacles to Anne's reunion with Wentworth. In addition, the "laws of nature are slightly suspended" (*AC*, p. 33), as they are in romance, permitting Anne to regain the bloom of youth. The ravages of time and suffering are wiped out, and the rejuvenated Anne is given the second chance for which we all long.

This combination of realism and romance accounts, I think, for much of *Persuasion*'s emotional impact. Anne's pain in the first half of the novel is given a serious rather than a comic treatment. The author does not keep us at a distance from her suffering or treat her plight in a way which assures us that it is only temporary. We see much of the action from Anne's point of view, and we become deeply involved in her emotions. The author herself lacks distance from Sir Walter and Elizabeth; she presents them satirically, but without amusement. Her hostility toward these characters, combined with Lady Russell's anxiety on Anne's behalf, heightens our sense of the gravity of Anne's situation. The fact that Anne retains her gentleness and dignity in the face of her difficulties enhances our admiration for her and intensifies our sense of the injustice of her fate. When, in Lyme, the most serious obstacles to her happiness are suddenly removed, we feel transported into a new literary universe. From this point on the novel works out a fantasy in which Anne's bargain with fate is justified and her noble qualities receive the reward which is their due. Our pleasure in this turnabout is so intense because the dangers to her have seemed so real.

Thematically, *Persuasion* has much in common with the earlier novels, though it also moves in some new directions. It is, like *Sense and Sensibility* and *Mansfield Park,* a novel in which the protagonist does not change. Anne is perfect from the beginning; the happy ending is dependent upon Wentworth recognizing that he has mistaken her character and giving her the love and appreciation which she has all along deserved. Anne is a synthesis of some of the most desirable qualities of the preceding heroines. She combines a discriminating mind with sweetness of manner and tenderness of heart. She lacks the buoyancy and charm of Elizabeth and Emma; but her behavior is invariably correct, as theirs is not; and she has deeper feelings than these more prestige-conscious women. The virtues which she displays are not new in Jane Austen, though their combination is.

Persuasion is a new departure principally in its emphasis upon the importance of individual exertion, its questioning of prudence, and its more favorable attitude toward world-openness, spontaneity, and romance. Wentworth is the most dashing of Austen's heroes, and his confidence in his ability to master fate is justified by events. Anne is guided by prudence in her youth, but she learns romance as she grows older. The naval people generally are characterized by informal, spontaneous manners which proceed from a genuine feeling for others. They have earned their place in the world through meritorious service; and they lead adventurous lives, the discomforts and dangers of which are compensated for by the variety and intensity of their experience. All of this sets them in contrast to Sir Walter and Elizabeth Elliot, who behave with "heartless elegance" (II, x), who do not deserve the position which they have inherited, and who lead empty, sterile lives, for which they are compensated by the preservation of their good looks. Instead of concluding with the heroine in a safe refuge, as Austen's novels usually do, *Persuasion* leaves Anne confronting the uncertainties of life. When she marries a naval officer, she is exposed to the risks of the profession and must live in "dread of a future war" (II, xii).

Though *Persuasion* is not nearly as rich in mimetic detail as the other novels which I have been considering, Anne Elliot is another of Jane Austen's memorable character creations. In addition to being a romantic heroine and an embodiment of almost all of the author's ideals, she is an imagined human being whose sufferings are all the more moving because they seem to be those of a real person. Her character traits are so unobtrusive, her problems seem so much the product of her situation, and the author's view of her is so compelling that no one has given much attention to the complexities of her personality. When we look at Anne as a person, it is evident that she has been hurt psychologically by her family's neglect and her frustration in love, and that many of her virtues are the product of her defensive strategies. She combines many of the qualities which Jane Austen admires in her earlier heroines because she combines their solutions: she is a mixture of detachment, compliance, and perfectionism.

2

A recurring feature of comedy, as Frye observes, is the "point of ritual death" *(AC,* p. 179). This is the point, usually near the end, at which the author brings "his action as close to the catastrophic overthrow of the hero as he can get it" *(AC,* p. 178). In some cases, the protagonist is actually in danger of death, while in others the love, fortune, or position which he desires seem impossible to attain. The tragic possibilities of the hero's plight are brought clearly into view and then are "dispelled so quickly that one has almost the sense of awakening from a nightmare" *(AC,* p. 179).

In *Persuasion,* the point of ritual death occurs in the first half of the novel rather than near the end, and it is unusually prolonged. Anne is in no danger of physical death, of course; but it seems that her chances of attaining love, recognition, and a meaningful place in society have been lost forever. She feels her life to be in its autumnal phase: "youth and hope, and spring" have "all gone together" (I, x). Captain Benwick is better off than she: " 'I cannot believe his prospects so blighted forever. He is younger than I am; younger in feeling, if not in fact; younger as a man. He will rally again and be happy with another' " (I, xi). As might be expected, these reflections occur just before the turnabout in Anne's fortunes which is produced by the return of her good looks and Louisa's fall on the Cobb.

Anne is in no way responsible for her own plight. She is a victim of unfortunate circumstances and of the humors of others. Her troubles begin when the death of her mother, by whom she was loved, leaves her at the mercy of Sir Walter and Elizabeth, who do not appreciate her at all. Her father treats her like a stepchild, her older sister ignores her for Mrs. Clay, and her younger sister exploits her. She has an appreciative friend in Lady Russell, but it is clear from the outset that the only way she can have a satisfactory life is to leave her father's home for one of her own. Marriage, however, seems out of the question. Her beauty has faded, her mind is fastidious, and her circle of acquaintance is small. Lady Russell begins "to have the anxiety which borders on hopelessness" (I, iv) about Anne's finding a suitable mate. The man whom she loves is looking for a wife, but he is ready to be charmed by almost any woman except Anne.

Anne had an opportunity for marriage when she was nineteen; but Wentworth lacked money, her father would not help her, and Lady Russell persuaded her to break off the engagement. Wentworth blames Anne for being weak; but from the author's point of view it is the humors of Sir Walter, of Lady Russell, and of Captain Wentworth himself which are responsible for her plight. Wentworth is the chief blocking force both to Anne's happiness and to his own. He could have married her as soon as his fortune was made; but he was prevented from repeating his offer by his pride, which was hurt, and by his mistaken conception of her character. His return to the neighborhood heightens her misery by reawakening her love while at the same time making it clear that they are to be perpetual strangers. Eventually, however, it is the means by which he is cured of his illusions; for it gives him the opportunity to see Anne's true worth and to understand the dangerous consequences of a headstrong temper.

The turning point of the comic action comes in the Lyme episode, which is unlike anything in Jane Austen's earlier novels. Her fiction belongs typically to Frye's third phase of comedy, which is closer to irony and satire than to romance, and in which the humorous society is replaced by a clearsighted one at the end. *Persuasion* belongs more to the fourth phase in which "we begin to move out of the world of experience into the ideal world of innocence and romance" *(AC,* pp. 181-82). The fourth phase may be called

> the drama of the green world, its plot being assimilated to the ritual theme of the triumph of life and love over the waste land. . . . Thus the

action of the comedy begins in a world represented as a normal world,
moves into the green world, goes into a metamorphosis there in which
the comic resolution is achieved, and returns to the normal world. *(AC,*
p. 182)

"The green world," says Frye, "charges the comedies with the
symbolism of the victory of summer over winter"; it has "analo-
gies, not only to the fertile world of ritual, but to the dream
world that we create out of our own desires" *(AC,* p. 183).

Lyme is clearly the green world. At the beginning of the
episode, Anne is living in an emotional wasteland. Her bloom
has faded, her younger rival is winning Wentworth, and she has
almost completely resigned herself to a life without love. Both
she and the season are in an autumnal state, and winter is fast
approaching. Her glimpse of the good society which is consti-
tuted by the naval characters only deepens her gloom because
she seems so irrevocably cut off from it and confined to the
sterile world of the Elliots. Then, with startling suddenness,
Anne is rejuvenated: "She was looking remarkably well; her
very regular, very pretty features, having the bloom and freshness of youth restored by the fine wind which had been blowing
upon her complexion, and by the animation of eye which it also
produced" (I, xii). She receives a look of "earnest admiration"
from William Elliot; and Captain Wentworth, who observes the
scene, once again finds her attractive. Captain Benwick is also
interested in Anne, and suddenly her life is full of romantic
possibilities. Her bloom remains with her when she returns to
the normal world. In receiving Lady Russell's compliments
upon her arrival at Uppercross, Anne connects "them with the
silent admiration of her cousin" and hopes that she is "to be
blessed with a second spring of youth and beauty" (II, i). Her
beauty is remarked upon frequently in Bath and is even noticed
by her father.

The restoration of Anne's beauty removes one major obstacle to the renewal of Wentworth's love, and Louisa's fall on
the Cobb removes the others. He had preferred Louisa's temperament to Anne's; but he is now forced to realize "that a
persuadable temper might sometimes be as much in favour of
happiness, as a very resolute character" (I, xii). Anne's compe-

tence in the emergency confirms his sense of her superiority, and he realizes that it is she whom he has loved all along. Because of his careless attentions, however, he is committed to Louisa. This difficulty, too, is removed in the green world of Lyme, when Louisa transfers her affections to Benwick.

The second half of *Persuasion* is a prolonged denouement in which Anne moves steadily in the direction of happiness. There are complications to be sure, but none of them are serious. The nightmare has lifted. Life and love have triumphed over the wasteland. Anne dreads going to Bath, where she has been unhappy before and where no one will "be glad to see her" (II, ii). But her family greets her cordially, and Mr. Elliot is very attentive. He is the chief threat to Anne's happiness in this part of the novel. He is an attractive man who appears to possess an ideal combination of gentlemanly qualities. He is Sir Walter's heir; and he is a favorite of Lady Russell, who earnestly wants Anne to marry him. He offers Anne an opportunity to escape her inconsequential position and to inherit the place of her mother. Despite all this, she is never seriously tempted. Her heart belongs to Wentworth, and her mind tells her that Mr. Elliott is not to be trusted. Once Wentworth is released from Louisa, the only real problem to be solved is that of communication. This occasions some interesting maneuvers by both the author and the lovers, but the issue is never in doubt.

Anne's happiness at the end seems almost complete. Although her relationship with Wentworth has illustrative importance, it is primarily a love story. Wentworth is the most virile of Jane Austen's heroes, and Anne is her most romantic heroine. There is more passion between these lovers than is customary in Austen's fiction. Their relationship is, moreover, relatively undefined, permitting us to project upon it our own romantic fantasies. They fall in love before the action begins, and the novel ends with their joyous reunion. It is difficult to detect any reason within the relationship why these lovers should not be happy. The chief threat to their happiness is the fear of a future war, but this is purely external.

At the end Anne wins not only Wentworth, but also the general admiration of her fellows and a place in the good society. At the beginning she has Lady Russell, but no one else either appreciates or cares about her. By the end she is the center of attention and is surrounded by admirers. The good society within which she finds a place is that of the naval people. In fourth phase comedy, the humorous society is not necessarily transformed, nor does a new society always emerge at the end. The action of the comedy may be presented, rather, "on two social planes, of which one is preferred and consequently in some measure idealized" *(AC,* p. 182). This is exactly what happens in *Persuasion.* The society of the Elliots remains essentially unchanged. Anne does not assume her proper place within it, but leaves it for a better society which has been there all along. The blocking characters are left to drag out their lives in a wasteland of their own making, while Anne enjoys the warmth and camaraderie of a circle of people who are distinguished at once for their national importance and their domestic virtues. She is joined by Lady Russell, her only true friend from the Kellynch world, who is included in the good society because she is able "to admit that she had been . . . wrong" about almost everything (II, xii).

3

The thematic structure of *Persuasion* is, as usual, a system of contrasts and balances. Anne Elliot is an embodiment of the golden mean between various extremes. She displays just the right combination of flexibility and firmness, of elegance and sweetness, of emotionality and self-control. Jane Austen's highly perceptive characters tend to lack warmth, but Anne is "tenderness itself" (II, xii). She is the standard by which the other characters in the novel are measured. It is her example, her perceptions, and her judgments which enable the reader to understand the virtues and defects of the other characters and to give them their proper place in the author's system of values. It is through Anne, moreover, that Austen explores the conflicting claims of prudence and of romance. This is the novel's central thematic issue and the source of much of its complexity and freshness.

The most striking contrast in the novel is, of course, between Anne and the other members of her family. Sir Walter,
Elizabeth, and Mary are vain, self-indulgent, superficial people
who are devoid of inner resources and who do not deserve the
privileged position which they enjoy. The irresponsibility of Sir
Walter and Elizabeth leads to the crisis in their affairs which
forces them to relinquish Kellynch. In contrast to these members of her family, Anne values honesty above importance and
substance over appearance. She is more concerned with the
duties of an aristocratic position than with the privileges which
it affords. After the departure of Sir Walter and Elizabeth,
Anne lives for a time with Mary; and we are given a vivid
picture of the differences between these sisters. Mary is selfish,
ineffectual, and dependent, whereas Anne is helpful, compe-
tent, and self-sufficient. "Inheriting a considerable share of the
Elliot self-importance," Mary is "very prone to add to every
other distress that of fancying herself neglected and ill-used"
(I, v). Anne *is* neglected and ill used, but she bears her fate
stoically and is equable and uncomplaining.

If Anne were the only foil to her father and sisters, *Persuasion* would constitute a devastating indictment of the upper
classes, especially since Anne joins the naval society at the end.
There are two other characters, however, who embody the
positive qualities of the aristocracy, though not as perfectly as
Anne, who shares their virtues but is free of their defects.
Anne's mother was a "sensible" woman whose "judgment and
conduct, if they might be pardoned the youthful infatuation
which made her Lady Elliot, had never required indulgence
afterwards" (I, i). She promoted the "real respectability" of her
husband for seventeen years; and though she was not the happiest of women, she "found enough in her duties, her friends,
and her children, to attach her to life." Anne, too, attempts to
promote the respectability of her family; and though she is
personally unhappy, she takes great satisfaction in fulfilling her
duties. She has learned from her mother's experience, however,
and does not repeat the error for which Lady Elliot must be
pardoned. She is exposed to a temptation similar to her mother's
in the attentions of Mr. Elliot; but she refuses to be captivated

by good looks, fine manners, and the prospect of a high social position.

Lady Russell is also an exemplar of aristocratic virtues. She possesses "strict integrity" and "a delicate sense of honour" (I, ii). She is "a benevolent, charitable . . . woman . . . ; most correct in her conduct, strict in her notions of decorum, and with manners that were held a standard of good breeding." Anne admires and shares all of these qualities, but she rejects Lady Russell's "prejudices on the side of ancestry" and her excessive respect for "rank and consequence." Lady Russell's aristocratic prejudices, when combined with her lack of "a natural penetration" in "the discernment of character" (II, xii), lead to mistaken judgments of both Captain Wentworth and Mr. Elliot and make her an unreliable guide to Anne in her relationships with these men. Anne differs from Lady Russell not only in her greater perceptiveness and her slighter regard for rank and consequence, but also in her ability to appreciate the qualities of people who are beneath them in the social order. Admiral Croft's manners, for example, "were not quite of the tone to suit Lady Russell, but they delighted Anne. His goodness of heart and simplicity of manner were irresistible" (II, i).

Anne is the bridge between the aristocratic world of her father and Lady Russell and the society of less elegant but worthy people like the Musgroves, the Harvilles, and the Crofts. Anne is jarred at times by the Musgroves' excessive informality and lack of refinement; but she envies the warmth and ease of their family circle; and she applauds the parents' attitude toward their childrens' marriages, which is free "from all those ambitious feelings which have led to so much misconduct and misery, both in young and old" (II, x). She is amused by the Crofts' style of driving, which is a good "representation" of the somewhat haphazard "guidance of their affairs" (I, x); but on the whole she has a strong admiration of these people. She relishes their gusto and spontaneity, and she recognizes their superiority to her own family in their human relations and their discharge of the duties which belong to the masters of Kellynch. Admiral Croft is a bit too simple to be her ideal of a man, but she takes Mrs. Croft as her model of a navy wife. She is altogether charmed by the Harvilles' warm hospitality and by their ability to make life cosy and cheerful in the midst of rather straightened circumstances. Whatever these people may lack in style or cultivation of mind is far outweighed by their genuineness, good will, and real delicacy of feeling; and Anne feels more at home with any of them than she does amidst the cold elegance of her family circle.

Captain Wentworth is for Anne, of course, the most attractive member of the naval society. Her termination of their enagement in response to Lady Russell's advice generates both the novel's plot and its thematic complications. This event raises three major questions: Was the advice good or bad? Was Anne right or wrong to have followed it? And, was Wentworth's response to Anne's behavior justified or not? Upon the correct answers to these questions depend the reconciliation of the lovers at the end, the vindication of Anne's character, and a proper understanding of the attitude toward life which Jane Austen is proposing in this novel.

If judged in terms of its consequences, Lady Russell's advice is clearly mistaken. Anne's life seems to have been ruined by her friend's counsel. Lady Russell remains "as satisfied as ever with her own discretion" and "never wish[s] the past undone"; but Anne thinks "very differently" at seven and twenty "from what she had been made to think at nineteen": "She did not blame Lady Russell, and she did not blame herself for having been guided by her; but she felt that were any young person, in similar circumstances, to apply to her for counsel, they would never receive any of such certain immediate wretchedness, such uncertain future good" (I, iv). Her thoughts are now "eloquent . . . on the side of early warm attachment, and a cheerful confidence in futurity, against that over-anxious caution which seems to insult exertion and distrust Providence!" Having been "forced into prudence in her youth," she has "learned romance" as she has grown older—"the natural sequence of an unnatural beginning."

These passages early in the novel create a distinct impression that Lady Russell's advice was wrong and that both Anne and the author have repudiated prudence in favor of romance. In the novel as a whole, however, Lady Russell's advice receives strong reinforcement; prudence is not so much repudiated as subjected to the test of experience, which shows it to be a problematic rather than an absolute value, and one which should sometimes be subordinated to faith and love.

Lady Russell's objections to the engagement derive in part, of course, from her aristocratic prejudices; and insofar as they do, they carry no weight with Anne and are meant to be rejected by the reader. Love is more important than a prestigious connection. The chief reasons for her opposition, however, make perfectly good sense. Wentworth has "no hopes of attaining affluence, but in the chances of a most uncertain profession, and no connexions to secure even his farther rise in that profession" (I, iv). He has made money in the past, "but spending freely, what had come freely," he has "realized nothing." He is "full of life and ardour" and is confident that his luck will continue. This is enough for Anne; but Lady Russell is distrustful of both his prospects and his "headstrong character"; and she fears that such an uncertain engagement will reduce Anne to "a state of most wearing, anxious, youth-killing dependance." It is, ironically, the termination of the engagement which kills Anne's youth; but Lady Russell's reasoning represents the conventional wisdom of her society and is in harmony with the value system of Jane Austen's earlier novels.

Lady Russell's position receives powerful support later in the novel, during the discussion of long engagements which takes place at the White Hart Inn:

> "Oh! dear Mrs. Croft," cried Mrs. Musgrove, . . . "there is nothing I so abominate for young people as a long engagement. . . . It is all very well . . . for young people to be engaged, if there is a certainty of their being able to marry in six months, or even in twelve, but a long engagement!"
>
> "Yes, dear ma'am," said Mrs. Croft, "or an uncertain engagement; an engagement which may be long. To begin without knowing that at such a time there will be the means of marrying, I hold to be very unsafe and unwise, and what, I think, all parents should prevent as far as they can." (II, xi)

Not only are these sentiments the same as Lady Russell's, but they are expressed by characters who give them great authority. Mrs. Musgrove is an indulgent parent who does not allow considerations of prestige or fortune to outweigh the happiness of her children, and Mrs. Croft is the only character in the novel who is Anne's equal in perceptiveness. As the two ladies continue to talk, they "re-urge the same admitted truths, and enforce them with such examples of the ill effect of a contrary practice, as had fallen within their observation."

Anne and Wentworth are present during this discussion. Anne feels its "application to herself . . . in a nervous thrill all over"; and Wentworth gives her a "quick, conscious look." It is evident that Anne feels vindicated by the favorable light in which Lady Russell's advice has been placed, and that Wentworth's understanding of Anne's behavior has been further clarified by his overhearing this conversation. Nevertheless, when she justifies herself to Wentworth a little while later, Anne does not say that Lady Russell " 'did not err in her advice. It was, perhaps, one of those cases in which advice is good or bad only as the event decides; and for myself, I certainly never should, in any circumstances of tolerable similarity, give such advice.' " Anne would not give such advice because, just as she was once persuaded that her engagement was "indiscreet," she is now "persuaded that under every disadvantage of disapprobation at home, and every anxiety attending his profession, all their probable fears, delays and disappointments, she should yet have been a happier woman in maintaining the engagement, than she had been in the sacrifice of it" (I, iv). She fully believes that this would have been so "had . . . even more than a usual share of all such solicitudes and suspense been theirs, without reference to the actual results of their case." Notice that Anne is presented as moving not from error to truth, but from one persuasion to another.

What Jane Austen is showing us is not the dangers of overanxious caution or even the need to find a happy medium between prudence and romance, but the inadequacy of "admitted truths" as a guide for every situation in life and the difficulty of knowing when to follow the established wisdom and when to listen to the promptings of the heart. One reason why life seems larger and more mysterious in *Persuasion* than it does in the earlier novels is that Austen is moving from a classical balancing of opposites toward a modern emphasis upon the relativity of values and the need to judge each case individually. This results in a sense of uncertainty which is quite different from the awareness of complexity which is produced by her antithetical structures. Mrs. Musgrove and Mrs. Croft have observed many examples of the ill effect of long or uncertain engagements; the accepted wisdom probably fits most cases. But in Anne's case it is nearly disastrous, and Anne would never give such advice "in similar circumstances" (I, iv). Anne's understanding of her own case, however, is the product of hindsight; and it is difficult to know whether she could correctly assess the circumstances of another person and guide him appropriately. Her advice, too, might prove to be good or bad only as the event decides.

Anne's justification of her own behavior in following Lady Russell's advice has aroused uneasiness in some readers; but from a thematic point of view, there are no real difficulties, especially when we see that the advice was, though wrong in the circumstances, well meant and usually sound. Anne's motives were prudence and duty. She came to feel that the engagement was indiscreet, not only for herself, but also for Wentworth: "The belief of being prudent, and self-denying principally for *his* advantage, was her chief consolation" (I, iv). Even though she was wrong in her judgment of what would be most advantageous, she was " 'perfectly right in being guided' " by Lady Russell, who was to her " 'in the place of a parent' "(II, xi). To have done otherwise would have been a violation of duty: " 'I should have suffered more in continuing the engagement than I did even in giving it up, because I should have suffered in my conscience.' "

We are here back in Austen's familiar world of fixed values. If prudence is sometimes more dangerous than romance, duty takes precedence over love; and its dictates are always certain. Anne is rewarded for her dutifulness by an authorial dispensation of justice which permits her both to have romantic fulfillment at the end and to maintain her self-approbation. Prudence is subjected to the realities of experience; but duty is still an absolute value, obedience to which brings happiness.

Persuasion, like all of Jane Austen's novels, depicts a process of education. In this case, the education is that of Captain

Wentworth, who must come to appreciate Anne's virtues and to understand his own faults. Lady Russell is not entirely wrong in her distrust of his character. It is his blindness and pride which are the chief sources of Anne's unhappiness and of his own. If he had renewed his offer when events gave him "the independence which alone had been wanting" (I, vi), Lady Russell's advice would have had no ill effect.

Wentworth's education is made possible by his renewed contact with Anne, which reminds him of her excellence, and by his involvement with Louisa Musgrove, which brings home to him the consequences of rashness and obstinacy. At first he is attracted by Louisa's " 'decision and firmness,' " which he contrasts to Anne's " 'too yielding and indecisive . . . character' " (I, x); but the accident on the Cobb places Louisa's resoluteness in a different light; and he learns "to distinguish between the steadiness of principle and the obstinacy of self-will, between the darings of heedlessness and the resolution of a collected mind" (II, xi). Wentworth has been heedless himself in his attentions to the Musgrove girls. He first threatens Henrietta's relationship with Charles Hayter; and, then, by his "excessive intimacy," he binds himself to Louisa. At the very time when he becomes aware of his renewed love for Anne, he becomes conscious also of the fact that he is " 'no longer at [his] own disposal' ": " 'I had been grossly wrong, and must abide the consequences.' " Wentworth blames himself also for Louisa's fall on the Cobb, which is "the consequence of much thoughtlessness and much imprudence" (II, i); " 'Oh God! that I had not given way to her at the fatal moment! Had I done as I ought!' " (I, xii).

Wentworth's self-assurance is treated with extraordinary sympathy early in the novel. He offers himself to Anne on a most insubstantial basis: "He had always been lucky; he knew he should be so still" (I, iv). His wit and ardor convert Anne, and Lady Russell is mocked for her "horror" of "anything approaching to imprudence." When his "sanguine expectations" are justified by success, Anne rejects overanxious caution in favor of "a cheerful confidence in futurity." Wentworth's education is typical, however, for an Austen protagonist. His aggressiveness serves him well in war, but it leads to serious errors in his human relations. His pride must be chastened, and he must undergo a good deal of self-castigation before he can be rewarded in love. Having been rescued from his mistakes through no merit of his own, he " 'must learn to brook being happier than [he] deserve[s]' " (II, xii). In his youth, Wentworth has a romantic belief in his ability to master fate; but he is forced to learn prudence and humility as he grows older. This provides the necessary contrast to Anne's development and is the natural sequence of a natural beginning.

Anne's movement in the direction of a greater openness to experience qualifies her to become a sailor's wife and to live with the risk and uncertainty which that entails. Wentworth's education in prudence and humility enables him to appreciate Anne and to be reconciled with Lady Russell. The union of Anne and Wentworth at the end combines the ardor of their earlier relationship with a substantiality which it lacked. They are "more exquisitely happy, perhaps, in their re-union, than when it had been first projected; more tender, more tried, more fixed in a knowledge of each other's character, truth, and attachment; more equal to act, more justified in acting" (II, xi).

4

Anne's childhood situation is similar to that of Elizabeth Bennet in that her family is divided into two camps. Anne is the favorite of the sensible parent, her mother; but she is unappreciated by her vain and foolish father. Whereas Elizabeth has her supportive parent as a constant ally, Anne loses her mother when she is fourteen. She still has her mother's friend, Lady Russell; but neither her father nor her older sister have any love for her; and she is subject, as a result, to mistreatment and neglect.

Anne expresses little resentment at the way in which she is treated, but the narrator and Lady Russell are frequently indignant on her behalf, and through them we are given a vivid sense of the deprivations and indignities which she endures. Anne was "nobody," the narrator tells us, "with either father or sister: her word had no weight; her convenience was always to give way;—

she was only Anne" (I, i). When Sir Walter informs his oldest daughter, during a stay in London, that they must retrench, Elizabeth has "the happy thought of their taking no present down to Anne." During the councils on the family's financial plight, Lady Russell does "what nobody else thought of doing, she consulted Anne, who never seemed considered by the others as having any interest in the question" (I, ii). When Sir Walter decides to take up residence in Bath, "the usual fate of Anne attended her in having something very opposite from her inclinations fixed on."

Lady Russell is full of vexation at the slights which Anne receives and is completely frustrated by her inability to influence Elizabeth and Sir Walter. She has been "repeatedly very earnest in trying to get Anne included in the visit to London" and is "sensibly open to all the injustice and all the discredit of the selfish arrangement which shut her out." She is quite disturbed by Elizabeth's coldness toward Anne, and especially by her "turning from the society of so deserving a sister" to that of Mrs. Clay. Elizabeth is eager to have Mrs. Clay accompany her when she moves, but she tells Anne that " 'nobody will want her in Bath' " (I, v). This affront is repeated in Bath, when Elizabeth assures Mrs. Clay, within Anne's hearing, that " 'she is nothing to me, compared with you' " (II, iv). The sight "of Mrs. Clay in such favour, and of Anne so overlooked, [is] a perpetual provocation to" Lady Russell. She is eager to see Anne married so that she will be "removed from the partialities and injustice of her father's house" (I, iv).

What is Anne's reaction to all those slights? How does she handle such abuse? One thing which should be noted is that Anne's reactions differ from those of Lady Russell. She seems to experience neither the pain nor the anger which her friend feels on her behalf, and she does not assert her rights or try to improve her situation. Lady Russell finds Elizabeth's preference of Mrs. Clay to be "a very sore aggravation"; but Anne, we are told, "was become hardened to such affronts" and is concerned only about "the imprudence of the arrangement" (I, v). As can be seen from this, Anne defends herself partly by detachment. She maintains an emotional distance from her family and tries not to care about their behavior toward her. The "patience and resignation" which she preaches to Captain Benwick have been learned partly from her frustration in love and partly from her experience at home. Her mother provided a model, no doubt, of "worth and suffering" which impressed upon her "the duty and benefit of struggling against affliction" (I, xi). Both Anne and her mother are low-spirited, oppressed women who glorify endurance and try to subdue their sensitivity. To be alive to their feelings is, for them, to suffer.

There is a good deal of submission mixed in with Anne's resignation. She stresses to Benwick not only the benefit, but also the duty of accepting suffering. Given the influence of her mother and the fact that she grows up in the shadow of her older sister, it is not surprising that Anne develops a number of self-effacing characteristics. She is modest, grateful, and un-complaining. She rejects ambition, represses envy, and is al-ways sympathetic with the feelings of others. Having received the message that she is "nobody," she tries to gain a sense of importance by utilizing every opportunity to be of service. When Mary insists that she remain at Uppercross while the others go to Bath, Anne is quite willing to comply: "To be claimed as a good, though in an improper style, is at least better than being rejected as no good at all; and Anne, glad to be thought of some use, glad to have any thing marked out as a duty . . . readily agreed to stay" (I, v). Her most cherished experience at Uppercross is "her usefulness to little Charles" when he dislocates his collarbone (I, xi). She performs other services as well, of course, such as mediating family squabbles, providing music at the Musgroves, and humoring Mary out of her fits of hypochondria and injured pride. She dislikes the tension of being asked to take sides, but she enjoys the feeling that at Uppercross she is at least of some importance.

Anne's self-effacing behavior is well illustrated in the epi-sode of the walk to Winthrop. The Musgrove girls initiate the plan. They do not want Mary, who tires quickly; but she becomes jealous and insists upon joining them. Anne at first tries to dissuade Mary; but when this fails, she feels it best to accept the girls' invitation to herself, "as she might be useful in turning back with her sister, and lessening the interference in any plan of their own" (I, x). Here, as elsewhere, Anne is motivated not by what she wants for herself, but by what will be of use to others. She seems to have accepted the idea that other people's feelings are important but that hers do not count. She adopts a retiring role when she is in company and sees her aim in life as service to others rather than self-fulfillment. Her object on the walk is to stay out of everybody's way, unless, of course, she is needed.

Anne's lack of anger and of self-assertion is not only the result of her detachment. Her self-effacing trends generate powerful taboos against all forms of aggressiveness, which are felt to be selfish. She can be assertive in the name of principle or of family respectability, but almost never in her own behalf. The reader is supposed to admire this as noble, but it is in reality compulsive. Her family's acceptance of her is so marginal that she cannot risk losing it by fighting for her rights. Anne's defensive strategies have a certain value, given her situation; but in many ways they are self-defeating. One reason why she fares so badly is that her compliance and resignation tend to invite continued exploitation and neglect. Her father and sisters are expansive people who have an exaggerated sense of the importance of their own wishes. Anne has been bullied by them into giving up too much.

Beneath Anne's gentle manner there is an accumulation of repressed resentment which is partly responsible for her chronic depression. This resentment is incompatible both with her idealized image of herself and with Austen's image of her. It is expressed in the novel not by Anne, but by Lady Russell and the narrator,[1] just as Fanny Price's pride in her own goodness is expressed by others. The submerged side of Anne is most clearly evident in her relationship with Captain Wentworth, whose expansiveness provides her with a vicarious fulfillment of her own aggressive drives. Anne is quick to detect Wentworth's amusement at Mrs. Musgrove's "large fat sighings" over her son Dick (I, viii), his contempt for Mary's snobbishness toward the Hayters (I, x), and his "disdain" when Elizabeth invites him to Camden-place (II, x). She is not indignant, but is sympathetic with his feelings, which parallel her own.

Though Anne is resigned to being unhappy and accepting abuse, she is by no means demoralized or crushed. She has pride, dignity, and self-respect. She is fastidious and discriminating and has a sense of superiority which compensates for her various deprivations. Anne contemplates the Musgrove girls "as some of the happiest creatures of her acquaintance" and envies their "good understanding" and "mutual affection"; "but still, saved as we all are by some comfortable feeling of superiority from wishing for the possibility of exchange, she would not have given up her own more elegant and cultivated mind for all their enjoyments" (I, v).

Anne's satisfaction with herself is derived in part from her natural abilities, which *are* superior to those of almost everyone else; but its primary source is the approval which she received during her formative years from her mother and Lady Russell. These women were the chief objects of her respect and her only source of emotional support, and they held her to a very high standard. While she lived, her mother provided Anne with an inspiring example of dutifulness and responsibility; and when she was dying, she relied on Lady Russell for the "maintenance of the good principles and instructions which she had been anxiously giving her daughters" (I, i). Lady Russell, as we know, was "most correct in her conduct" and "strict in her notions of decorum" (I, ii). Anne was the favorite of both of these women in part, no doubt, because she followed their example. When we meet her as an adult, she is as dutiful as her mother and as "consciously right" in her "manners" as Lady Russell (II, v). Lady Russell is devoted to culture, and so is Anne. If Anne deviates from her models, it is only to avoid their deficiencies and mistakes.

By the time Anne has grown up, her standards are completely internalized. She is a perfectionist whose self-approval matters more to her than anything else. She may be unappreciated by almost everyone around her; but as long as she lives up to her lofty standards, she has a "comfortable feeling of superiority." She has more pride than the other members of her family; for she cannot enjoy Lady Dalrymple's welcome, which depends " 'so entirely upon place' " (II, iv). Anne's place has never entitled her to much consideration, which may be one reason why she does not give a high value to rank. Her claims are based upon personal merit, and the only recognition which she values is that of other superior people who are able to appreciate her worth.

However hungry she is for affection or oppressed by the injustices of her father's house, Anne will not betray her principles or her sense of worth by marrying indiscriminately. After her engagement to Wentworth is broken off, "no second attachment" is "possible to the nice tone of her mind, the fastidiousness of her taste, in the small limits of the society around them" (I, iv). Charles Musgrove proposes, but he is too ordinary a person for a woman like Anne. The most striking example of her fastidiousness is, of course, her decision that she could never marry Mr. Elliot even before she knows that Wentworth is free and before she hears Mrs. Smith's story. Her objections to this enormously attractive match are purely moral:

> He certainly knew what was right, nor could she fix on any one article of moral duty evidently transgressed; but yet she would have been afraid to answer for his conduct. She distrusted the past, if not the present. . . . She saw that there had been bad habits; that Sunday-travelling had been a common thing; that there had been a period of his life (and probably not a short one) when he had been, at least, careless on all serious matters; and, though he might now think very differently, who could answer for the true sentiments of a clever, cautious man, grown old enough to appreciate a fair character? How could it ever be ascertained that his mind was truly cleansed? (II, v)

This is an amazing piece of analysis given the scantiness of the evidence and Anne's vested interest in thinking well of a man whose attentions have been so flattering. It shows, I think, the overwhelming importance to her of moral perfection.

Anne copes with her situation, then, through a combination of defenses. She moves away from Sir Walter and Elizabeth, and from her own feelings of frustration and resentment. This reduces her pain, but it also saps her vitality. She moves toward those who value her or allow her to be of service. She is of so little importance at home and her life is so empty that she has an almost pathetic need to be needed. Her primary defense, however, is neither resignation nor compliance. It is the perfectionism which she derives from Lady Elliot and Lady Russell, and which gives her a strong sense of rectitude and superiority. Because it is combined with powerful self-effacing trends,

Anne's perfectionism has a milder appearance than does that of Jane Austen's other self-righteous characters. Anne is accomplished but modest. She combines "fortitude and gentleness" (II, xi), "a strong mind, with sweetness of manner" (I, ii).

It is now possible to understand Anne's attraction to Captain Wentworth, her termination of their engagement, her subsequent loss of bloom, her reactions to Wentworth's return, and the process of rebirth which begins with her experiences in Lyme. At the time of their first encounter, Wentworth is "a remarkably fine young man, with a great deal of intelligence, spirit, and brilliancy" (I, iv). His intelligence marks him as a superior person, and his spirit and brilliance are immensely appealing to a girl whose own spirits have been low since the death of her mother. Anne feels like an outcast, a stepchild of fortune. Wentworth has already been lucky, and he is confident of his ability to master fate. Through her identification with him Anne can escape from the feeling of impotence by which she has been oppressed. He offers her the rescue from without which is her only hope. He gives her the love and admiration for which she is yearning. He sees in her the "highest perfection." She has had "hardly any body to love," but now she will be able to lavish upon him all of her devotion. It is no wonder that she is in a state of "exquisite felicity" and that "young and gentle" as she is, she is prepared "to withstand her father's ill-will" to maintain the engagement.

The opposition of Lady Russell is, of course, quite another matter. Since the death of her mother, Lady Russell has been her only "truly sympathizing friend" (I, vi); and it is frightening to Anne to be in conflict with her. To defy Lady Russell in this matter is tantamount, moreover, to defying her mother; for she has been bequeathed, as it were, to Lady Russell, who has "almost a mother's love, and mother's rights" (I, iv). Both her self-effacing and her perfectionistic shoulds demand submission to maternal authority. Anne can think of withstanding her father's ill-will because he does not actually prohibit the match, because there is no affection here to be lost, and because there are no reasons for his opposition which she can respect. Some of Lady Russell's reasons, however, are difficult for her to resist. By conventional standards, the engagement is, after all, imprudent. It does not seem so to Wentworth, with "his sanguine temper, and fearlessness of mind"; but Anne has neither his optimism nor his self-confidence; and she is "persuaded to believe the engagement a wrong thing—indiscreet, improper, hardly capable of success, and not deserving it." Her belief that it does not deserve success indicates that a certain amount of guilt has been generated by the emergence of her self-assertive impulses. Once she concludes that the engagement is wrong, she must relinquish it, of course, in order to protect her pride in her own rectitude. She maintains her image of herself as loving and unselfish by imagining that she is "consulting [Wentworth's] good, even more than her own."

For a brief time, during her engagement, Anne abandons her resignation and permits herself to experience hope and joy. The dissolution of the engagement is a crushing blow which leaves her more depressed than she has ever been before. She follows Wentworth's fortunes and hopes that his early success will bring a renewal of his attentions. When it does not, she is hurt; but she is not angry, despite the fact that she feels that he is being unfair to her. Even when he returns and treats her as a stranger, she is not resentful at his coldness; nor is she highly critical of his careless behavior toward the Musgrove girls. Her only concern is for his honor and the happiness of the other parties. Lady Russell's heart revels "in angry pleasure, in pleased contempt, that the man who at twenty-three had seemed to understand somewhat of the value of an Anne Elliot, should, eight years afterwards, be charmed by a Louisa Musgrove" (II, i). This is another instance of Lady Russell's experiencing feelings which are missing in Anne. Anne's repression of all negative feelings toward Wentworth indicates, among other things, the intensity of her identification with him. She is still experiencing his triumphs vicariously and is protecting her pride in his original choice of her. She has adopted the heroic role of the long-suffering woman whose life has been ruined by the mistakes of others, but who blames no one, and who continues to love when hope is gone.

Anne represses her negative feelings toward Lady Russell also. She knows that Lady Russell meant well and gave the conventional advice, but this advice has ruined her life, and it is difficult to believe that she feels no resentment. She has too much need of Lady Russell, who is now truly her sole resource, to allow herself to experience her anger. The fact that she never discusses the Wentworth affair with Lady Russell indicates that she is afraid of the subject; and her refusal to blame her friend has the look of a reaction formation. She punishes Lady Russell in an indirect way by excluding her from her innermost life. When Charles Musgrove proposes, she leaves "nothing for advice to do" (I, iv). She is obviously unhappy, but she will not share her feelings. Lady Russell's resulting state of anxiety gives her, no doubt, a secret satisfaction.

Although Anne does not blame Lady Russell, she does allow herself to repudiate her friend's advice. The strength of her feelings on this subject indicates that it is a focus for her frustration and resentment. Prudence is a value which looks to the future. It is the voice of the reality principle which tells us to delay gratification in order to avoid undesirable consequences and to secure a safer, though more distant, happiness. In Anne's case, there was nothing to wait for, nothing to protect. The evils attending the engagement would have been far more acceptable than the consequences of its dissolution. Anne's is the perspective of a woman who feels that her life is over and who is oriented toward the missed opportunities of the past. Her romantic attitude reflects her longing for love and the courage of despair. Like her author, who was dying while she wrote this book, Anne has a greater openness toward life now that all seems lost. Her readiness to take risks should not be confused, however, with a weakening of her principles. Her sense of duty remains as strict as ever; and insofar as prudence involves moral considerations, and not simply those of personal interest, her commitment to it is unchanged.

Before Captain Wentworth's return, Anne is in a state of "desolate tranquillity" (I, v). She has no prospects for happiness, and her feelings are blocked in almost every direction. The initial effect of Wentworth's reappearance is to revive the conflict between hope and resignation. The news that the Crofts have rented Kellynch creates an intense "agitation," which she tries to dispel by telling herself that it is "folly" (I, iv). She is so excited during her first meeting with Wentworth that she begins to "reason with herself" in an effort "to be feeling less": "Eight years, almost eight years had passed, since all had been given up. How absurd to be resuming the agitation which such an interval had banished into distance and indistinctness!" (I, vii). Her efforts at detachment are of little avail, however; and she is soon asking herself the meaning of Wentworth's appearance at her sister's: "Was this like wishing to avoid her?" The "next moment," however, she is "hating herself for the folly which asked the question." Her hopes are crushed when she hears that Captain Wentworth has found her "altered beyond his knowledge." Painful as it is, she is glad to have heard these words: "They were of a sobering tendency; they allayed agitation; they composed, and consequently must make her happier."

We see here Anne's habitual method of combating anxiety and maintaining her peace of mind. Longings for fulfillment are dangerous to her, since they can only bring frustration and despair. When such feelings arise, she tells herself that they are absurd or foolish and she hates herself for having them. Her self-hate is generated by the violation of her detached shoulds, which seek to make her invulnerable by prohibiting hope and desire. When Wentworth rescues her from the pesterings of little Walter, Anne is "ashamed of herself, quite ashamed of being so nervous, so overcome by a trifle" (I, ix). This is the shame of failing to live up to one's idealized image. Her defensiveness persists even later, when her hopes are by no means unreasonable. Upon learning that Wentworth is "unshackled and free," she has "some feelings which she [is] ashamed to investigate. They were too much like joy, senseless joy!" (II, vi). And when, shortly thereafter, she "starts" at the sight of Wentworth on the street, she feels that she is "the greatest simpleton in the world, the most unaccountable and absurd!" (II, vii).

The major change which Anne undergoes in the course of the novel is the lifting of her resignation, and, with it, the inner deadness which has been the price of her tranquillity. This process begins in Lyme, where she emerges from obscurity at last and gains recognition. Captain Benwick seeks her out for companionship and advice, and Captain Harville is most grateful for her service to his friend. Under the influence of fine weather and congenial people, her looks begin to improve; and they are noticed by Mr. Elliot, whose interest in Anne draws the attention of Captain Wentworth. In the confusion following Louisa's fall, everyone turns to her for direction. When Louisa must be left behind, Captain Wentworth wishes her to stay— " 'No one so proper, so capable as Anne' " (I, xii). She has the satisfaction of reflecting that her character has been vindicated in relation to Louisa's. On the journey back to Uppercross, Wentworth shows "deference for her judgment" in deciding how to break the news to the Musgroves; and during her stay at Uppercross, Anne has "the satisfaction of knowing herself extremely useful there" (II, i). Mrs. Musgrove has never paid much attention to Anne's services, but her "real affection [is] won by her usefulness when they [are] in distress" (II, x). Everyone is in dread of her departure: " 'What should they do without her?' " (II, i).

These are highly significant experiences for a woman like Anne, who has for so long been deprived of admiration, esteem, and a sense of importance. With her confidence somewhat restored, she begins to dream about the possibilities of happiness. When Lady Russell compliments her on her looks, she has "the amusement . . . of hoping that she [is] to be blessed with a second spring of youth and beauty" (II, i). Her amusement indicates that she is still maintaining a protective detachment, but her hope is real. She looks forward to a possible visit from Captain Benwick, whose compliments have been repeated by Charles Musgrove; and she feels that she would like to know more about Mr. Elliot. Captain Wentworth seems bound to Louisa, but she feels confident now of his esteem. When she goes to Bath, she feels "that she would rather see Mr. Elliot again than not, which was more than she could say for many other persons in Bath" (II, ii). Now that she has people who are interested in her, she can afford to feel some of her resentment toward her family, and she becomes more critical of them than she has been before.

Anne's spirits steadily rise as good things continue to happen. Mrs. Croft treats her as a favorite (II, i), her family is unexpectedly cordial (II, iii), and Mr. Elliot courts her assid-

uously, preferring her to her sister Elizabeth, whom she now
begins to outshine. Tributes pour in from all sides to her elegance, beauty, and worth. Most important of all is the love of
Captain Wentworth, which offers her not only romantic fulfillment, but also a confirmation of her sense of superiority.
Before they reach an understanding, she tries to protect herself
by being "wise and reasonable" (II, vii); but she finds this
increasingly difficult to do. When she sees at the concert that
Wentworth is jealous of Mr. Elliot, "the gratification [is] exquisite" (II, viii); and her musings the next morning are "of
high-wrought love and eternal constancy" (II, ix). As she strives
to remove obstacles and to establish communication between
herself and Wentworth, she becomes active, as never before, in
the pursuit of her own wishes. When Wentworth proposes, she
is euphoric. His letter produces "an overpowering happiness";
and when they meet on the street, their "spirits" dance in
"rapture" (II, xi).

Anne's improved fortunes lead her to abandon her resignation, but her other strategies remain much the same. Her
euphoria results in part from the fact that her self-effacing and
perfectionistic claims are being honored and her dreams of
glory are coming true. Anne is still modest, unambitious, and
ready to serve. When the Musgroves arrive, she "naturally
[falls] into all her wonted ways of attention and assistance"
(II, x). At her father's evening party, she is "more generally
admired than she thought about or cared for" (II, xi). Her
"high-wrought felicity" creates an anxiety against which she
defends herself by feelings of gratitude: she becomes "steadfast
and fearless in the thankfulness of her enjoyment." Her felicity
lies in "the warmth of her heart" (II, xii) and in the merging of
her own identity with that of the expansive Wentworth. "She
glorie[s] in being a sailor's wife."

Anne's perfectionism is most clearly in evidence in her
conversations with Wentworth. She corresponds to his (and the
author's) ideal of a woman: she combines "a strong mind, with
sweetness of manner" (I, vii). When she ends their engagement, however, he feels that she has given him up "to oblige
others"; and this indicates "a feebleness of character . . . which
his own decided, confident temperament [can] not endure. He is

an expansive person who is repelled by what he takes to be Anne's excessively compliant behavior. What he must come to see is that she is really a resolute woman who made her decision on the basis of principle, and not because of weakness. His acknowledgment of his error is the theme of his lovemaking at the end, where he dwells as much upon Anne's "merits" as upon her feminine attractions. Her character is "now fixed on his mind as perfection itself" (II, xi). These tributes to her excellence are as important to Anne as his professions of love. Despite all his praise, however, Anne is not content. She must prove both to herself and to him that she was " 'perfectly right' " to have been guided by Lady Russell and that no blame attaches to her whatsoever. " 'I have now,' " she concludes, " 'as far as such a sentiment is allowable in human nature, nothing to reproach myself with.' " This statement shows that, despite a strong admixture of self-effacement, Anne is predominantly a perfectionistic person. It is an open expression of pride from which a Fanny Price would shrink.

Despite this contrast between the heroines, *Persuasion* more closely resembles *Mansfield Park* than it does any other novel. Both novels are Cinderella stories, and both glorify the defenses which the heroines develop in response to being abused. In both the heroines are misunderstood, and in both they are vindicated. The difference is that Fanny is proved to be perfectly good, whereas Anne is proved to be perfectly right. Both novels are fantasies in which the heroine's predominant solution seems to be failing but is ultimately triumphant. It seems that Anne has sacrificed love for duty, but she gains a greater happiness at the end as a result of her rectitude. In both novels the protagonists are realistically portrayed throughout, while their problems are removed by the author's manipulation of the plot.

6

Jane Austen:
The Authorial Personality

1

We know many of the facts of Jane Austen's life; but there is little evidence, outside of her writings, of her attitudes, values, and beliefs, and of the dynamics of her personality. Her letters, after Cassandra's excisions, are not highly revealing; and she did not move among literary people who could have left us penetrating accounts of her character. I believe that we can learn a good deal about Jane Austen by analyzing the personality which can be inferred from all of her fiction. I shall call this her authorial personality to distinguish it from the implied authors of her individual novels and from the historical person, who had a life independent of her artistic creations.

I shall analyze Austen's authorial personality with the aid of Horneyan psychology, which, as I have shown, is congruent with a great many aspects of her fiction.[1] This approach will lead me to focus, of course, upon those phenomena to which it is well suited. I do not rule out the use of other psychological theories, which may reveal different aspects of Austen's personality; but, for the most part, I have left that task to others. Though I shall draw upon a general knowledge of Austen's life when I try to trace her development from novel to novel, my portrait of her is based primarily upon what can be learned from her fiction; and I shall make no attempt to trace the etiology of her character or to integrate my findings with the biographical data. To do so would require a separate study.

We must be careful, of course, when making inferences about an author from his fictions. We must allow for artistic motivations, for the requirements of the genre and of the *telos* of the individual work. A writer of comedy does not necessarily believe that the real world operates according to the mythos of Spring, and works of art have an inner logic of their own which often takes the author in unexpected directions. Still, we can learn much about an author from his works by examining such things as his recurring preoccupations, the personal element in his fantasies, the kinds of characters he creates, and his rhetorical stance. Although Jane Austen's authorial personality may not be identical in all respects with that of the historical person, it provides the richest source of insight into her character structure and her inner life.

Horneyan psychology can help to illuminate the author through his works because in the course of artistic creation the author's defensive strategies tend to express themselves in a variety of ways. His works are, among other things, efforts to reinforce his predominant solution and to resolve his inner conflicts by showing himself, as well as others, the good and evil consequences of the various trends which are warring within him. He will tend to glorify characters whose strategies are similar to his own and to satirize those who embody his repressed solutions. His rhetoric will affirm the values, attitudes, and traits of character which are demanded by his dominant shoulds, while rejecting those which are forbidden by his major solution. His plots will often be fantasies in which his claims are honored in a magical way, while his repressed strategies are shown to bring misery and retribution. Because he cannot help expressing his subordinate trends, however, his works will frequently manifest his inner conflicts. His attitudes, values, and beliefs will often be inconsistent or self-contradictory. His conflicting shoulds will lead him to criticize each solution from the point of view of the others and to have toward his characters the mixed feelings which he has toward the aspects of himself which they embody. The relationships among his solutions may vary, moreover, in the course of his life; and this will be reflected in changes in the kinds of characters he portrays, in his rhetoric, and in his dominant fantasies.

All of this may seem readily applicable to a tormented artist like Dostoevsky, but of dubious relevance to so poised a novelist as Jane Austen. A look at the criticism reveals, however, that there are fierce disagreements about Austen's true character. As I have observed, some critics emphasize the aggressive, satirical component of her art; some stress her gentleness and conservatism; and some focus upon the detached, ironic quality of her vision. A psychological analysis of Austen's authorial personality will show how these diverse components of her nature are related to each other within a structure of inner conflicts.

2

The major unvarying element in Jane Austen's fiction is a code of values and conduct that serves as the norm by which all deviations are satirized and judged. The code is not always what the fiction is primarily about, and different aspects of it are explored in different works; but it is almost always present in one form or another, and no character gains Austen's sympathy or approval who does not either subscribe to it from the beginning or come to feel its force at some point in his development. Austen associates the code at various times with such influences as religion, education, and example; but it is often embraced in the absence of good training, desirable models, or the support of the surrounding community. It has the independent authority of self-evident truth. Those who are faithful to it seem to be innately superior to their fellows in intelligence, disposition, or rationality. Experience is important, however; for some well-endowed people are irremediably corrupted by bad influences, while others need to err and suffer in order to be purged of their faults.

The code embraces six major areas of life: family relations, courtship and marriage, friendship, everyday social intercourse, duties to oneself, and duties to the community. Different aspects of the code are operative for different individuals, depending upon their age, sex, economic status, and social and familial roles; but its general principles are always the same. The values which it endorses include prudence, judgment, good sense, self-knowledge, sensitivity, perceptiveness, propriety, civility, self-control, sincerity, integrity, respect for authority, dutifulness, responsibility, unselfishness, consideration of others, self-denial, humility, gratitude, moderation, patience, fortitude, tenderness, generosity, warm feeling, domestic affection, and the sanctification of marriage by love and mutual esteem. Deviations from the code result from selfishness, stupidity, ill-nature, self-indulgence, pride, ambition, materialism, vanity, or commitment to a competing code which glorifies opposite values.

One competing code is that which is associated with the cult of sensibility. Austen ridicules it in the *Juvenilia,* most notably in "Love and Freindship," and subjects it to serious criticism in *Sense and Sensibility.* In "Love and Freindship," Laura not only ignores, but consciously scorns proper values and takes an intense pride in her own false standards. She is boastful, self-indulgent, ungrateful, dishonest, irresponsible, and insensitive to the rights of others. She judges by externals, falls in love at first sight, and marries her hero within an hour of their meeting. She wears her "sensibility too tremblingly alive to every affliction of [her] Freinds, [her] Acquaintance and particularly to every affliction of [her] own" as a badge of honor.[2] She has contempt for the few sensible characters she encounters (see pp. 83, 93, 100-101) and worships those who share her own perverted code of values. Her husband, Edward, is a model of filial impiety. " 'It is my greatest boast,' " he proclaims, " 'that I have incurred the displeasure of my Father!' " (p. 85). Her friends, Augustus and Sophia, are self-absorbed (p. 87), improvident, and dishonest. They "scorned to reflect a moment on their pecuniary Distresses and would have blushed at the idea of paying their Debts" (p. 88). Sophia ultimately dies from her excess of sensibility. When Edward and Augustus are killed in an accident, Sophia faints "every moment" and Laura runs mad "as often" (p. 99). Sophia falls ill from lying insensible in the damps of the night and is carried off in a few days by a galloping consumption. " 'Run mad as often as you chuse,' " she advises her friend as she expires, " 'but do not faint—' " (p. 102).

Marianne Dashwood's faults are far less extreme, of course. She is a good-hearted and intelligent girl who has been led astray by the ethic of sensibility, which is reinforced, for her, by the example of her mother. It is a matter of pride to her to disdain prudence, to set propriety at nought, to refuse the duties of civility, and to indulge in her emotions of joy and grief without restraint. She comes close to sharing Sophia's fate; and her brush with death, combined with the example of Elinor, leads her to see the error of her ways:

> "I saw in my own behavior . . . nothing but a series of imprudence towards myself, and want of kindness to others. I saw that . . . my want of fortitude . . . had almost led me to the grave. . . . Whenever I looked toward the past I saw some duty neglected, or some failing indulged. Everybody seemed injured by me. . . . I have laid down my plan, and if I am capable of adhering to it, my feelings shall be governed and my temper improved. They shall no longer worry others, nor torture myself. I shall now live solely for my family. . . . if I do mix in other society, it will be only to show that my spirit is humbled, my heart amended, and that I can practice the civilities, the lesser duties of life, with gentleness and forbearance." (Ch. 46)

Jane Austen was fascinated with the cult of sensibility because, as a powerful literary and social phenomenon, it posed an important challenge to what she regarded as right values and the proper conduct of life. With the completion of *Sense and Sensibility,* she seems to have lost interest in it as a major subject for her fiction and to have turned her attention to other objects of satire. Her attitude toward it does not change, however; and in *Persuasion* she once again defines her own position toward it in a way which is reminiscent of her earlier treatment.

Anne Elliot, like Elinor Dashwood, suffers and feels intensely but never loses her self-control or her sensitivity to others. She is set against such characters as her sister Mary, Louisa Musgrove, and Captain Benwick, who display some of the typical failings of high-strung or self-indulgent sensibility. Anne combines, more fully perhaps than any other protagonist, the virtues of the code heroine with the romantic feelings which are supposed to be the exclusive province of the heroine of sensibility. She is more romantic, in the final analysis, than the melancholy Benwick, and more self-disciplined and useful besides. Lady Russell, in her description of Mr. Elliot, defines the characteristics of the code hero and their relationship to the hero of sensibility in a way which can serve, despite the inaccuracy of her application, for all of Jane Austen's fiction:

> he judged for himself in every thing essential, without defying public opinion in any point of worldly decorum. He was steady, observant, moderate, candid; never runaway with by spirits or by selfishness which fancied itself strong feeling; and yet, with a sensibility to what was amiable and lovely, and a value for all the felicities of domestic life, which characters of fancied enthusiasm and violent agitation seldom really possess. (II, vi)

This could serve, with few changes, as a description of Colonel Brandon or Edward Ferrars. It is not sensibility to which Austen objects, but sensibility which is exaggerated, affected, or out of control. Deep feeling is part of the code, but so is its regulation and appropriateness to the occasion.

The most serious violations of Austen's code result not from the excesses of sensibility, but from worldliness. This involves, in essence, the callous pursuit of money, power, and prestige. The code of worldliness sanctions such values as pride, ambition, snobbery, acquisitiveness, manipulativeness, the pursuit of competitive triumph, cunning, hypocrisy, exploitation of the opposite sex, and marriage for wealth and status rather than for love. The softer feelings are ignored or scorned as a sign of weakness, and self-interest is worshipped as the highest good. There are varying degrees of worldliness, of course; and not all worldly characters display the whole range of vices. Some basically good characters are tainted by worldly attitudes (Sir Thomas Bertram, for example); and only a few characters (such as Jane Bennet and Fanny Price) are presented as being entirely

173

free of them. Some characters are quite blatant in their worldliness, and some are unconscious of it. Others, usually the villains, are hypocritical and maintain a pretense of commitment either to sentimental values (Willoughby) or to the true code. Anne Elliot perceives, as Lady Russell does not, that Mr. Elliot may be playing a role. Who can "answer for the true sentiments of a clever, cautious man, grown old enough to appreciate a fair character?" (II, v). When the whole truth comes out, she sees him for what he is, "a disingenuous, artificial, worldly man, who has never had any better principle to guide him than selfishness" (II, ix).[3]

3

It is possible to analyze the competing codes in Jane Austen from a psychological point of view. The cult of sensibility glorifies infantile self-indulgence and adolescent rebellion. The heroes and heroines of sensibility pursue immediate gratification, reject all restraint, and display an adolescent defiance of convention and authority. They refuse to look out for themselves or to accept responsibility for others. They demand that the world be indulgent, mothering, and magically responsive to their needs. In their human relations, they rely upon feeling rather than upon judgment. They respond enthusiastically to people who seem like kindred spirits and react coldly to those who represent caution and morality. They are poor at all forms of reality testing. They tend to be helpless, gullible, and dependent, the victims of their own unregulated impulses and of other, more worldly people. They are selfish and sometimes dishonest, but in a childish rather than in a calculating way. They have a naive belief in their right to have what they want, and they blame others for their frustrations or the unpleasant consequences of their indiscretions. Whatever their own excesses, they have a sense of militant innocence.

From Austen's point of view, as well as from my own, the cult of sensibility represents a form of immaturity, of fixation at an early stage of development. It occupied her attention most fully when she was young, when the central issue of her life must have been whether she was going to grow up or to remain a child. Even in the *Juvenilia* she treats it from a mature perspective, but she may have been so absorbed by it because it posed a temptation which had to be overcome if she was to live up to her own image of maturity. She is less interested in it after *Sense and Sensibility,* where Marianne's conversion represents the triumph of adulthood, though most readers feel a sense of loss, as she may have herself, at all of that liveliness gone out of the world.

Worldliness, on the other hand, is a subject which she found to be of more enduring interest. It appears in her work as early as "The Three Sisters" *(Volume the First),* and it is never far from the center of her satiric attention. It represents the temptations of adult life: the temptation to give up one's idealism, to be corrupted by too much wealth and power, by the pressures of adaptation to harsh realities, or by the perverted values of a competitive society. In some cases, however, worldliness is another form of immaturity. Many of Austen's worldly characters are spoiled children who have never had to struggle and endure, or ambitious people who cannot accept their natural place in society but are too self-indulgent to rise through honest effort.

It is rewarding to analyze certain aspects of Austen's work in primarily Freudian terms. Her heroes and heroines of sensibility are people under the domination of the pleasure principle who refuse to adapt themselves to natural and social laws. The code of worldliness can be seen as a rationalization of primitive impulses of lust and aggression. The true code, on the other hand, stresses the values of the ego and the superego. In her most appealing work, Jane Austen seems to be looking for a way to grant as much libidinal satisfaction as is compatible with the demands of reality and the moral imperatives. With the exception of Fanny Price, the code heroes and heroines tend to have strong egos; they cope better than most people and combine good sense and high morality with strong feelings and a desire for personal fulfillment. The moral of Austen's stories seems to be that there is more happiness to be gained by being prudent and principled than by succumbing to the temptations of worldliness or desire. The pleasure principle must not dominate, but much satisfaction can be attained via the detour through reality. Jane Austen writes comedy, to be sure; but it is comedy for adults.

Much more could be said along Freudian lines, but I shall leave that task to others. It is from a Horneyan perspective that I wish to approach the majority of Austen's characters and the psychological structure of her authorial personality as a whole. Many of her worldly characters can be readily understood as Horney's aggressive or expansive types, and her code heroes and heroines have either perfectionistic or self-effacing personalities. She herself displays leanings in all three of the Horneyan directions, and she has rather mixed attitudes toward all but the perfectionistic solution.

The code of worldliness is remarkably parallel to Horney's description of certain aspects of the aggressive personality. For the aggressive person, says Horney, "a callous pursuit of self-interest is the paramount law."[4] He needs "to achieve success, prestige, or recognition in any form." Consideration, compassion, loyalty, and self-sacrifice are scorned as signs of weakness; those who value such qualities are his natural victims. What he wants from his relations with the opposite sex is not love, but a sense of triumph. His prime concern in friendship or marriage is to connect himself with someone "through whose attractiveness, social prestige, or wealth he can enhance his own position." He despises soft feelings in himself and in others; but he is drawn to compliant people, nevertheless, because they give him a sense of power and control. He takes great pride in his ability to manipulate others and needs to do so in order to reinforce his sense of mastery. His aggressive attitudes are sometimes quite apparent, but often they are "covered over with a veneer of suave politeness, fair-mindedness, and good fellowship." He plays at conforming to accepted notions of goodness in order to carry out his private aims. "No such 'front' is necessary to the compliant type because his values coincide anyway with approved-of social or Christian virtues."

As we contemplate this composite picture of aggressive people, a number of Jane Austen's worldlings come to mind, each of whom conspicuously displays one or more of the distinguishing traits. They include Isabella and John Thorpe and Captain and General Tilney from *Northanger Abbey;* Mrs. John Dashwood, Mrs. Ferrars, Robert Ferrars, Lucy Steele, and Willoughby from *Sense and Sensibility;* Lady Catherine, Miss Bingley, and Wickham from *Pride and Prejudice;* Mrs. Norris, Mary and Henry Crawford, and Tom and Maria Bertram from *Mansfield Park;* Mr. and Mrs. Elton from *Emma;* and Sir Walter, Elizabeth, Mr. Elliot, and Mrs. Clay from *Persuasion.* Most of these characters are one-dimensional, though some, like Willoughby and the Crawfords, have a degree of complexity and are troubled by inner conflicts. Of them all, only Tom Bertram is salvable. There are several protagonists, of course (Elizabeth Bennet, Darcy, and Emma), who also display aggressive traits. Expansiveness is combined in their cases with other, more desirable characteristics. They undergo a process of education which consists largely in the crushing of their pride and the replacement of expansive with self-effacing attitudes. I am omitting for the moment a discussion of Austen's perfectionistic people. They also belong to the expansive category, but they must be considered separately.

Jane Austen's most remarkable portrait of a ruthlessly aggressive person occurs not in the novels, but in an early work, "Lady Susan," whose heroine is a forerunner of Becky Sharp. The work is epistolary in form; and there are some extremely revealing letters from Lady Susan to Mrs. Johnson, a confidante who shares her code and with whom Lady Susan is perfectly frank.

Lady Susan is a recently widowed beauty of about thirty-five who has a reputation as "the most accomplished Coquette in England."[5] As the story opens, she has been staying for several months with her friends the Manwarings, where she has made the "whole family miserable" (p. 248). She is having an affair with the husband and has subverted the affections of Sir James Martin from Miss Manwaring in order to marry him to her daughter, Frederica, who frustrates her plan by refusing the match. When things become too uncomfortable at Langford, she visits her brother-in-law, Charles Vernon, at Churchill, leaving her daughter at an expensive school in London, where she will learn to be reasonable and will make good connections:

"The price is immense, and much beyond what I can ever attempt to pay" (p. 246).

The visit to Churchill is a rather desperate measure, for it is situated in "that insupportable spot, a Country Village" (pp. 245-46); and the Vernons have good reason to be hostile, since Lady Susan had been opposed to their marriage. Mrs. Vernon has a sharp eye for hypocrisy and is difficult to deceive; but Charles is a compliant type who is easily taken in: "Disposed . . . as he always is to think the best of everyone, her display of Greif, & professions of regret, & general resolutions of prudence were sufficient to soften his heart, & make him really confide in her sincerity" (p. 247). Lady Susan "really [has] a regard for him, he is so easily imposed on!" (p. 250). She plans to win her "Sister-in-law's heart through her Children; I know all their names already, & am going to attach myself with the greatest sensibility to one in particular, a young Frederic, whom I take on my lap & sigh over for his dear Uncle's sake" (p. 250). Mrs. Vernon, however, sees through her facade:

> Her address to me was so gentle, frank & even affectionate [she writes to her mother], that if I had not known how much she has always disliked me for marrying Mr. Vernon, & that we had never met before, I should have imagined her an attached friend. One is apt I believe to connect assurance of manner with coquetry, & to expect that an impudent address will necessarily attend an impudent mind; . . . but her Countenance is absolutely sweet, & her voice & manner winningly mild. I am sorry it is so, for what is this but Deceit? . . . She is clever & agreable . . . & talks very well, with a happy command of Language, which is too often used I believe to make Black appear White. She has already almost persuaded me of her being warmly attached to her daughter, tho' I have so long been convinced of the contrary. (p. 251)

The main action of the story is Lady Susan's triumph over Reginald De Courcy, Mrs. Vernon's brother, who knows Lady Susan's past and visits Churchill with the expectation of amusing himself at her expense: "by all that I can gather, Lady Susan possesses a degree of captivating Deceit which must be pleasing to witness & detect. I shall be with you very soon" (pp. 248-49). Lady Susan meets his insolent familiarity with a "calm dignity of . . . deportment" which soon convinces him that she has been badly maligned: "I never behaved less like a Coquette in the whole course of my Life, tho' perhaps my desire of dominion was never more decided. I have subdued him entirely by sentiment & serious conversation" (pp. 257-58). While Reginald's sister and parents suffer in helpless agony at his thralldom, Lady Susan is delighted by her vindictive triumph: "There is exquisite pleasure in subduing an insolent spirit, in making a person pre-determined to dislike, acknowledge one's superiority" (p. 254).

Lady Susan's plans are seriously threatened when Frederica, upset by her mother's insistence upon her marriage to Sir James, attempts to run away from school and must be brought to Churchill for closer supervision: "I had not a notion of her being such a little Devil before; she seemed to have all the Vernon Milkiness" (p. 268). Frederica *is* a compliant type; but, like Fanny Price, she is adamant about not marrying a man whom she can neither love nor respect. When Sir James arrives at Churchill to pursue his suit in person, Frederica takes the desperate step of writing a note to Reginald De Courcy, enlisting his support. Reginald is so upset with Lady Susan's response that he prepares to leave; but she reverses herself and convinces him that there has been no real quarrel, only a misunderstanding. She scorns Reginald for his weakness, but is delighted to find him so tractable: "There is something agreable in feelings so easily worked on. Not that I . . . would for the world have such myself, but they are very convenient when one wishes to influence the passions of another" (p. 293).

"I am again myself," she writes to Mrs. Johnson, "gay and triumphant" (p. 291). She has taken some blows, however, and is full of schemes for vindictive triumphs:

> I have many things to compass. I must punish Frederica, & pretty severely too, for her application to Reginald; I must punish him for receiving it so favourably, & for the rest of his conduct. I must torment my Sister-in-law for the insolent triumph of her Look & Manner since Sir James has been dismissed . . . & I must make myself amends for the humiliations to which I have stooped within these few days. (p. 294)

She thinks, in fact, of bringing Frederica to London ("always the fairest field of action") and forcing her to marry Sir James; for it is not until her own will is effected, contrary to his, that she will deserve "some credit for being on good terms with Reginald" (p. 294).

Lady Susan fares in the end about as well, or as ill, as Jane Austen's other worldly characters. She loses Reginald when he accidentally encounters Mrs. Manwaring and learns the truth of the persisting rumors. She marries Sir James, a man whom she had earlier rejected for herself as too "contemptibly weak" (p. 245), and has such happiness as this sort of union can afford. She allows Frederica to live at Churchill, where, in due time, she and Reginald De Courcy are united.

Lady Susan displays an extreme form of worldliness, just as Laura and her friends represent the extremes of sensibility. But Laura is a caricature, whereas Lady Susan is a well-drawn mimetic character; and she has much more in common with the worldlings of the novels, such as Wickham and Mr. Elliot, than Laura has with Marianne Dashwood. Austen's antagonists are usually stock characters who are portrayed almost entirely from the outside, as befits the requirements of the works in which they appear. "Lady Susan" shows that Jane Austen could do such characters from the inside as well and gives us a better idea of the range of her psychological intuitions.

Jane Austen has, as I have indicated, a mixed attitude toward the expansive solution. As a rule, unreformed expansive characters fare badly in her novels; and it is against aggressive traits, values, and modes of behavior that she directs her most serious satire. There are ambivalences, however, and exceptions. The Crawfords have great vitality and charm; and Austen seems afraid, at times, of being seduced by their dangerous glamor. This is why she must treat them so harshly at the end and insist upon their inferiority to characters who are dull but good, like Fanny and Edmund. She portrays Emma's narcissism with unfailing insight and irony, showing both its destructiveness to others and its inadequacy as a means of dealing with life. But her mockery is gentle and sympathetic; and Emma is zestful, charming, and, indeed, even lovable, in her faults.

Captain Wentworth is the most successful of Austen's heroes, partly because he is the least fully developed and therefore does not escape his functional roles, and partly because he is a strong, masterful, self-assertive male who can inspire a romantic devotion such as Anne's and whom one can imagine to be an exciting lover. He must acknowledge his misjudgment of Anne and his mistake in not proposing again as soon as his fortune permitted; but his confidence in his ability to master fate is borne out by events, and Lady Russell's prudential fears are shown to have been unfounded. He is openly ambitious, and he pursues his fortune by a series of aggressive conquests. These are justified, of course, by the ethic of war. He serves, however, not primarily from a feeling of duty, but out of a lust for gain and an evident zest for adventure. As a naval man, he is similar to William Price, who receives completely favorable treatment.

The eligible young men in Austen's novels seem to fall into three main categories: those who are aggressive but not good, those who are good but unglamorous, and those who are aggressive and good enough. The last group includes Darcy and Wentworth, who are good enough to qualify them for the approval of the discriminating heroines, but whose appeal lies more in their expansive than in their moral qualities. With all of her insistence on goodness and her criticism of expansive values, there seems to be a longing in Jane Austen for aggressive triumph, primarily through a talented, masterful, and socially desirable man.

This longing comes out most vividly in *Pride and Prejudice,* in which Elizabeth gains the power and the glory of a grand marriage. Expansive people cannot achieve happiness in Austen's world until they have been brought down. Their pride must be crushed and they must be overwhelmed with self-criticism before they are worthy to be rewarded. This process is present in *Pride and Prejudice,* but in a muted form. Both Elizabeth and Darcy transfer their pride to each other, but their humility is a passing phase. Each admires the other more for his expansive than for his self-effacing qualities; and each looks to the other for the reinforcement of his pride. In order to reconcile the triumph of these two expansive types with her conscious values, Jane Austen makes it seem through her rhetoric that their happiness is the result of their having been properly humbled.

Austen's characters can be divided, as a number of critics have observed, into the simple and the complex. The simple characters tend to be either good or bad, self-effacing or aggressive. They are humors characters who do not change. The complex characters can be either wholly or predominantly bad, a mixture of good and bad, or wholly good. Those in the first group are incorrigible, those in the second are frequently capable of becoming wholly good through education, and those in the third group provide the norm by which everyone else is measured. The incorrigible characters are the self-consciously aggressive types who present a facade of goodness. The mixed characters often combine with their good qualities undesirable elements of aggressiveness or detachment. They may be extremely perceptive but deficient in feeling, or they may be seduced by feelings of a proud or an erotic nature into misperceptions and deviations from the code.

Just as Jane Austen has the most scorn for the complex bad characters, so she has the greatest admiration for the complex good ones. There are four complex characters who display an undeviating allegiance to the true code: Elinor Dashwood, Fanny Price, George Knightley, and Anne Elliot. Elinor and Knightley embrace the code in a predominantly perfectionistic manner; Fanny adopts it as part of her self-effacing solution; and Anne becomes a code heroine out of both self-effacing and perfectionistic motivations. To the degree that mixed complex characters embrace the code, they tend to do it for perfectionistic or self-effacing motives, or some combination of both.

Perfectionism is the only solution which Austen seems to identify with consistently. It is never an object of satire; and it is never the solution of the simple good characters who are sources of humor and who are treated both sympathetically and with an amused condescension. It is, of course, one of the expansive solutions; and it has in common with the others a need for superiority, recognition, and the mastery of life. It is different, however, in that it embraces noble standards rather than the self-serving ones of the other aggressive solutions. This makes it look, at times, like compliance; but while it shares many of the values of the self-effacing solution, it entertains them out of different motivations. Whether it be in the area of social behavior, intellectual astuteness, or ethical performance, the perfectionistic person needs "to attain the highest degree of excellence."[6] He identifies himself with his lofty standards and feels superior because of them. He makes strenuous efforts to live up to his shoulds and demands that others do so as well. The imposition of his standards on others leads to admiration for a select few and a critical or condescending attitude toward most of mankind. He conceals his contempt from others, however, because he should always be polite, and from himself as well, because "his very high standards prohibit such 'irregular' feelings." He wants others to recognize his rectitude, but the most important thing in his life is his self-approbation.

The perfectionistic person has a legalistic conception of the world order. Through the height of his standards, he compels fate. His claims are based

> on a "deal" he has secretly made with life. Because he is fair, just, dutiful, he is entitled to fair treatment by others and by life in general. This conviction of an infallible justice working in life gives him a feeling of mastery. His own perfection therefore is not only a means to superiority but also one to control life.

Because being right is so important to him, he has strong self-justifying tendencies. He experiences a sense of triumph when he is vindicated by events; and he takes great satisfaction in the acknowledgment by others of his good judgment, astuteness, or moral virtue. His recognition of "an error or failure of his own making. . . . pulls the ground away from under him. . . . Self-effacing trends and undiluted self-hate, kept in check successfully hitherto, then may come to the fore." I have shown how this pattern works with Emma.

Jane Austen's authorial personality often strikes me as being perfectionistic. She identifies completely with her perfectionistic characters, empathizes with their plight, and shares many of their traits. Her novels are an affirmation of her own high standards and a criticism of those who do not live up to them. The novels frequently leave the impression that life consists of a few exceptional people, like Austen herself, living in a world which is made up principally of knaves and fools. Her superior people are the lonely upholders of correct values who rarely encounter their equals in intelligence and virtue. They are consoled, however, by their self-approbation and are repaid by their eventual vindication and triumph. Her comic resolutions prove that her standards were correct and show that fidelity to them is rewarded by fate. They demonstrate the validity of her bargain: if people live up to their perfectionistic shoulds, their claims will be honored. She looks down upon her inferior characters, including the simple good ones, with amusement or contempt. Her irony is often a means by which she enjoys a sense of power and reaffirms her own superiority by making us aware of the limitations of her creatures. She is least ironic in those novels which contain code heroines; for she can display through them the characteristics of superior knowledge, finer values, and greater perception. Where a code heroine is not present or does not appear until the end, the implied author herself is more likely to engage in an overt display of perfectionistic trends.

Sense and Sensibility is the first of Jane Austen's fictions in which the true code is explicitly affirmed, and it is also her most elaborate celebration of perfectionism. Elinor is not as fully drawn as the later heroines, but she is a mimetic character who can be best understood through an analysis of her perfectionistic trends. She is shown to be invariably right. Marianne's education consists in learning from Elinor's example, as well as from experience, and in being converted to her sister's standards. Living, as Elinor does, in a family with opposite values and in a world of mental and moral inferiors, she is at first a rather lonely and unappreciated figure; but she converts her mother and sister, acquires a small band of admirers, and can look forward at the end to a satisfying existence in the midst of her happy few. Edward's rectitude is for a long time the major obstacle to Elinor's happiness and his own; but all of the protagonists, including Colonel Brandon and the reformed

Marianne, are ultimately rewarded. Willoughby learns that he could have been both happy and rich had he behaved with honor.

Sense and Sensibility seems to ask: how should a superior person like Elinor cope with an imperfect world in which she suffers from social injustice, the scarcity of peers, frustration in love, and unappreciative or disagreeable acquaintances? The answer seems to be that she should remain superior: she should live up to her own high standards and take satisfaction in her own moral and intellectual excellence.

Elinor takes great pride in the accuracy of her perceptions, the justness of her emotions, and the propriety of her behavior. She is almost constantly engaged in a subtle kind of self-congratulation and in an inward criticism of others. Her low opinion of mankind is indicated by her feeling as she departs from London that she is leaving "no creature behind from whom it would give her a moment's regret to be divided for ever" (Ch. 42), and even more by her remark that in marrying Lucy Steele, Edward will wed " 'a woman superior in person and understanding to half her sex' " (Ch. 37). Despite her frustrations, Elinor cannot be made really miserable as long as her pride in herself is intact. When she learns of Edward's engagement to Lucy, she feels resentment at first; but this quickly turns to pity for Edward and pride in her own rectitude and self-control: "Supported by the conviction of having done nothing to merit her present unhappiness . . . she thought she could even now, under the first smart of the heavy blow, command herself enough to guard every suspicion of the truth from her mother and sister" (Ch. 23). She urges the stricken Marianne to adopt a similar defense: " 'It is a reasonable and laudable pride' " to deprive others of their triumph by showing " 'how nobly the consciousness of your own innocence and good intentions support your spirits' " (Ch. 29). Colonel Brandon, who is in many ways Elinor's male counterpart, hopes that Marianne will be consoled by comparing her situation to that of his charge Eliza, who has been seduced by Willoughby: " 'She will feel her own sufferings to be nothing. They proceed from no misconduct and can bring on no disgrace' " (Ch. 31).

Elinor's defense renders her invulnerable to profound psychological suffering and offers a powerful compensation for external frustrations by giving her an inward sense of glory. It turns painful situations into occasions for triumph. When she learns of the engagement, she is "firmly resolved to act by [Lucy] as every principle of honour and honesty [direct], to combat her own affection for Edward and to see him as little as possible" (Ch. 23). Every subsequent encounter with Lucy is at once a painful exacerbation of her feelings and a source of profound moral satisfaction. She not only demonstrates her nobility, but she also thwarts Lucy's desire for triumph by showing that she cannot suffer because her heart is pure. Her heroism reaches its height when Edward calls upon her in London at the same time that she is receiving a visit from Lucy. She takes great pains to say all the proper things despite the awkwardness of the situation and "the consciousness of some injustice toward herself."

> Her exertions did not stop here; for she soon afterwards felt herself so heroically disposed as to determine, under pretence of fetching Marianne, to leave the others by themselves; and she really did it, and *that* in the handsomest manner, for she loitered away several minutes on the landing place, with the most high-minded fortitude, before she went to her sister. (Ch. 35)

I would suspect this passage of irony if there were anything else in the novel to support such an interpretation, but there is not. In addition to providing her with a romantic conception of herself as a heroine of duty, Elinor's defense also gives her a sense of controlling her fate. She assures Marianne that she wishes Edward to be happy; " 'and I am so sure of his always doing his duty, that though now he may harbour some regret, in the end he must become so' " (Ch. 37).

One of the mysteries of *Sense and Sensibility* is why so superior a person as Elinor Dashwood is attracted to Edward Ferrars. Edward is a shy, morose, inarticulate man, full of self-hate and inferiority feelings, who behaves incorrectly by attaching Elinor when he is already engaged, and who cannot be very perceptive if he supposes Lucy Steele "to be a well-disposed good-hearted girl and thoroughly attached to himself" (Ch. 49).

186

Elinor forgives him for his improper attentions because they are flattering to herself and because she knows that Edward did not mean to deceive. We have to take her word for his intelligence and sensitivity, something which not many readers have been willing to do. The chief basis of his appeal is that he appreciates her, which few others do, and that he is, like herself, absolutely committed to the code, even though his feelings and perceptions occasionally betray him. The highest praise of Edward comes, strangely enough, from Marianne; and it explains, as nothing else can do, Elinor's esteem:

> "And I really believe he *has* the most delicate conscience in the world; the most scrupulous in performing every engagement, however minute, and however it may make against his interest or pleasure. He is the most fearful of giving pain, of wounding expectation, and the most incapable of being selfish of anybody I ever saw." (Ch. 35)

Edward's goodness is of a self-effacing rather than of a perfectionistic sort, but the effect is the same. His diffidence and dutifulness become in Elinor's mind his "modesty and worth" (Ch. 36). Elinor consoles herself in her disappointment not only with her own rectitude, but also with his. It is important for her to feel that he has "done nothing to forfeit her esteem" (Ch. 23); for if he had, she would have to feel that she had misjudged him. When he sacrifices friends and fortune in order to honor his engagement, Elinor "glorie[s] in his integrity" (Ch. 38).

As we have seen, the code can be embraced in two ways; and *Sense and Sensibility* illustrates them both. Elinor's rectitude is the product of her perfectionism, while that of Edward and Marianne results from self-effacing tendencies. Marianne is the first of Jane Austen's heroines to undergo a conversion, that is, to have her self-effacing trends brought to the fore, as a result of the suffering which is consequent upon her errors. In the midst of her illness, she becomes eager " 'to live, to have time for atonement to my God, and to you all' " (Ch. 46). Her " 'spirit is humbled [and her] heart amended' "; she " 'cannot express [her] own abhorrence of [her] self.' " She is determined to make up for the past and to avoid future self-hate by giving up her self-indulgent way of life and devoting herself to others:

187

" 'I shall now live solely for my family.' " She finds fulfillment in her marriage to Brandon by living for him:

> Colonel Brandon was now as happy as all those who best loved him believed he deserved to be; in Marianne he was consoled for every past affliction; her regard and her society restored his mind to animation, and his spirits to cheerfulness: and that Marianne found her own happiness in forming his, was equally the persuasion and delight of each observing friend. (Ch. 50)

Her goodness is rewarded by the gratification of her romantic feelings: "Marianne could never love by halves; and her whole heart became in time, as much devoted to her husband, as it had once been to Willoughby."

I have given in the preceding chapters of this book a good deal of emphasis to the importance of the self-effacing solution for Jane Austen, to her support of its values, indulgence of its claims, and approval of the character traits associated with it. The education pattern in her novels is almost invariably one in which some form of excessive pride, self-indulgence, or worldliness is purged by suffering and example and replaced by self-effacing attitudes. Two of her paragons, Fanny and Anne, display self-effacing traits, in Fanny's case of an extreme kind. There are, in addition, a number of minor characters who are clearly self-effacing and whom Austen treats with considerable sympathy and admiration. Except in *Mansfield Park,* however, she seems to have a much more mixed attitude toward the self-effacing solution than she has toward the perfectionistic one. The self-effacing traits of her complex people are always regarded with respect, but her simple good people are often treated with a certain amount of irony, ridicule, or amused condescension.

Self-effacing types first appear in the *Juvenilia,* where they are objects of ridicule. The very first item in *Volume the First,* "Frederick & Elfrida," presents Charlotte Drummond, a friend of Elfrida, "whose character was a willingness to oblige every one" (p. 4). While she is visiting her aunt in London, the door suddenly opens and "an aged gentlemen with a sallow face & old pink Coat" throws himself at her feet, "partly by intention & partly thro' weakness," declares his attachment, and beseeches "her pity in the most moving manner." "Not being able to resolve to make anyone miserable, she consented to become his wife; where upon the Gentleman left the room and all was quiet" (p. 8). She is next entreated by "a young & Handsome Gentleman with a new blue coat." Since "the natural turn of her mind" is "to make every one happy," she promises "to become his Wife the next morning." The next morning she recollects "the double engagement" she has entered into and throws herself "into a deep stream which [runs] thro' her Aunt's pleasure Grounds in Portland Place" (p. 9). The hero of the piece, Frederick, is of a similarly compliant disposition. When he announces his intention of marrying another woman, Elfrida is "in such a hurry to have a succession of fainting fits, that she [has] scarcely patience enough to recover from one before she [falls] into another" (p. 11).

> Tho', in any threatening Danger to his Life or Liberty, Frederic was as bold as brass yet in other respects his heart was as soft as cotton & immediately on hearing of the dangerous way Elfrida was in, he flew to her & finding her better than he had been taught to expect, was united to her Forever—. (pp. 11-12)

The compliant type often appears in eighteenth century fiction as a variant of the hero of sensibility, namely, the benevolent gentleman. Jane Austen reduces this type to absurdity in "Evelyn" *(Volume the Third),* which tells of a village in Sussex named Evelyn where everyone is amiable, benevolent, and happy. A Mr. Gower becomes so enchanted with the place while passing through that he longs to settle in the village, but no house is available. His landlady tells him of a family, the Webbs, " 'who tho' warmly attached to the spot, yet from a peculiar Generosity of Disposition would perhaps be willing to oblige you with their house' " (p. 181). He calls upon the Webbs and receives from the mistress the warmest of welcomes: " 'Welcome best of Men—Welcome to this House, & to everything it contains.' " She then offers Mr. Gower her purse, apologizing for its inadequacy and assuring him that her husband has " 'cash in the house to the amount of an hundred pounds, which he shall bring you immediately.' " Mr. Webb enters the room and repeats "every protestation of Freindship & Cordiality which his Lady [has] already made."

> "And now my good Sir, said Mr. Webb, when Mr. Gower's repast was concluded, what else can we do to contribute to your happiness and express the Affection we bear you. Tell us what you wish more to receive, and depend upon our gratitude for the communication of your wishes." "Give me then your house & Grounds; I ask for nothing else." "It is yours, exclaimed both at once; from this moment it is yours." The Agreement concluded on and the present accepted by Mr Gower, Mr Webb rang to have the Carriage ordered, telling William at the same time to call the Young Ladies.
>
> "Best of Men, said Mrs. Webb, we will not long intrude upon your Time."
>
> "Make no apologies dear Madam, replied Mr Gower, You are welcome to stay this half hour if you like it."
>
> They both burst forth into raptures of Admiration at his politeness, which they agreed served only to make their Conduct appear more inexcusable in trespassing on his time." (Pp. 182-183)

In Jane Austen's realistic fiction, there are many simple characters of the self-effacing type. Charles Vernon, in "Lady Susan," is the epitome of his family's "Milkiness" (p. 268). He has a "generous temper" (p. 252), thinks the best of everybody, is easily deceived, and "live[s] only to do whatever he [is] desired" (p. 311). His closest counterpart in the novels is Bingley in *Pride and Prejudice*, who finds an equally compliant mate in Jane. The largest array of such characters is in *Emma*, where Miss Bates, Isabella, Mr. Woodhouse, Mr. and Mrs. Weston, and Harriet Smith all display one or more of the distinguishing traits of the self-effacing personality.

Jane Austen has a complicated attitude toward these simple self-effacing types. Their ingenuousness allures her as the opposite of worldly cynicism and selfish calculation. She admires their tender-heartedness, amiability, and freedom from conceit. They are good-natured, well-meaning, and ready to serve. They are easily pleased, grateful, and uncomplaining. Her complex mixed characters often feel inferior or guilty before them. Elizabeth feels that Jane's " 'sweetness and disinterestedness are really angelic' " and that she has never done her justice or loved her as she deserves (II, i). Emma is convinced for a while that Harriet is superior to herself "and that to resemble her would be more for her own welfare or happiness than all that genius or intelligence could do" (I, xvii). Austen seems to long at times to be like them herself, to share their simple, unconscious life. When Isabella leaves for London, Mr. Woodhouse returns to "his lamentations over the destiny of poor Isabella;—which poor Isabella, passing her life with those she doated on, full of their merits, blind to their faults, and always innocently busy, might have been a model of right feminine happiness" (I, xvii).

The chief deficiency of these people is that they are, after all, unconscious. They do not really understand themselves or others, and they lack discrimination. They approve too much, are too easily pleased, and tend to distort reality in order to maintain their rosy picture of the world. In dealing with worldly people, they are easily taken in. They are more fitted for suffering or obedience than for self-assertion or the exercise of authority. Though they are firm in the defense of their principles, they are in other respects too yielding, too complying, too weak.

Austen always treats these characters kindly, but many of them are humors at whom she is also laughing and for whom she cannot help feeling a touch of contempt. Like many of her complex characters, she has a great deal of pride invested in her understanding, her discernment, her elegant and cultivated mind. She delights in her powers and finds her genius and intelligence to be a rich source of satisfaction. She tends to see her simple compliant people from a perfectionistic point of view. She reverences their goodness; but she has a higher regard for people like herself who are not only good, but consciously so, and mentally superior as well. She knows, however, that the good simple kind have some qualities in which she is deficient, such as generosity, tender-heartedness, and humility; and she feels them to be her betters in these respects.

Marvin Mudrick sees Jane Austen as primarily detached. "Distance," he contends, was her "first condition for writing. She could not commit herself. . . . she allowed herself no public response except the socially conventional or the ironic; for

neither of these endangered her reserve, both put off self-com-
mitment and feeling, both maintained the distance between
author and reader, or author and subject: both were, primarily,
defenses." Her most characteristic defense is irony: "she maintained her distance by diverting herself and her audience with
an unengaged laughter." When she conforms to convention, it
is not out of commitment or principle, but out of a need to
conceal her subversive attitudes under the guise of compliance
and to maintain a rigid control over her own passionate impulses. "Irony and social forms are good because they enable
[her] to remain detached, from [her] self as from others; and
feeling is bad because it is a personal commitment."[7]

As my preceding analysis indicates, I believe that Austen
was firmly committed to her code. I agree with those critics who
argue that she "affirms society, ideally considered as a structure
of values . . . at the same time as she distinguishes it from its
frequently corrupted form";[8] that " 'principles' or 'seriousness'
are essential" to her art, since "there can be no true irony"
unless "there is something about which the author is never
ironical";[9] and that on the irony which comes from moral
detachment "she has made her own judgment in the figure of
Mr. Bennet, whose irony of moral detachment is shown to be
the cause of his becoming a moral nonentity."[10] There is a good
deal of detachment in Jane Austen, of course; but she is not
equally distant from all of her material. Her distance varies in
proportion to the degree to which her characters embody the
values, character traits, and forms of behavior which are sanctioned by the code. She has little or no distance from her wholly
good or "educated" complex characters. Sexual passion and
other unregulated feelings are dangerous not because they involve commitment, as Mudrick argues, but because they lead to
self-indulgence, faulty judgment, and other violations of the
code. A vivid example of this is Edmund Bertram, whose principles qualify him to be a code hero, but whose passion for
Mary Crawford leads him to misjudge her character completely
and to descend from his "moral elevation" (I, xvii) by partici-
pating in the play. Too much feeling is a threat not principally
to detachment, but to the tyrannical shoulds of the self-effacing

and perfectionistic solutions. Deep, serious, but regulated feelings are called for both by the code and by the self-effacing solution.

Though it is not Austen's predominant trait, detachment is important as a motif in her fiction and as a component of her authorial personality. Several detached values are included in the code, and the novels contain a number of characters who have marked tendencies in the direction of aloofness, withdrawal, or resignation. They include Henry Tilney, Elinor Dashwood, Elizabeth Bennet, Mr. Bennet, Charlotte Lucas, Fanny Price, Sir Thomas and Lady Bertram, Emma, and Anne Elliot. Austen has mixed feelings toward the various aspects of detachment, as she has toward all of the solutions except perfectionism.

We can see how detached values form part of the code most clearly in Elinor Dashwood and Anne Elliot. Both of these women have great personal reserve and take pride in their self-command. They have strong feelings of sorrow and of joy which they keep under control and do not like to show others. Elinor has moral reasons, of course, for not wanting to distress her family while she is inwardly grieving over the loss of Edward; but she is equally restrained when Marianne is declared to be out of danger and when she learns that it is Robert rather than Edward who has married Lucy Steele. Marianne's recovery "was an idea to fill her heart with sensations of exquisite comfort, and expand it in fervent gratitude; but it led to no outward demonstrations of joy, no words, no smiles. All within Elinor's breast was satisfaction, silent and strong" (Ch. 43). When she hears of Edward's freedom, she bursts "into tears of joy," but only after she has "almost [run] out of the room" in order to be alone (Ch. 48). She does not actually run out of the room, of course, for that would itself be excessively demonstrative; she only walks rapidly. It is evidently a matter of pride, of honor, of decorum to be strong and silent. Jane Austen seems to have a contempt for those who expose their emotions to the world. It should be noted, however, that candor and openness are also positive values, especially when they are displayed by the good simple types. There seems to be a conflict within the code between the detached values of reserve and self-sufficiency and the self-effacing values of emotional directness and intimacy.

The detached solution values not only self-control and the preservation of privacy, but also resignation, patience, and fortitude. We reduce our dependence on others by not needing them, by feeling "stronger alone" *(Sense and Sensibility,* Ch. 23); and we increase our independence of fate by bearing bravely the slings and arrows of outrageous fortune. Elinor is contrasted with Marianne, of course, in her ability to sustain misfortune. In *Persuasion* the contrast is between the stoicism of Anne Elliot and the shallow, self-indulgent, and demonstrative grief of Captain Benwick. Anne points out to him "the duty and benefit of struggling against affliction" and preaches "patience and resignation" (I, xi). It is often difficult to distinguish between a self-effacing acceptance of suffering and stoical resignation. It seems to me that Anne is an example of the latter, while Mrs. Smith illustrates the former. Mrs. Smith's misfortunes are of such a magnitude that mere resignation will not serve; and her cheerfulness suggests that she has glorified her suffering in a way which is alien to the detached solution. In Austen's value system, Mrs. Smith's solution is decidedly superior, while Anne's provides only a desolate tranquillity. In assessing Austen's attitude toward resignation we must recognize, moreover, that the governing fantasy of the novel is one which dispenses with the need for resignation, rather than one which celebrates its virtues.[11] In short, Austen admires Anne for her stoical fortitude, but she sees it as inferior to Christian submission and as a subordinate solution only in a world governed by Providence. Fate, for good people, is not ultimately unkind.

Jane Austen explores a different aspect of resignation in her portrait of Charlotte Lucas. Charlotte is to be admired for making the best of her unpromising marriage, but it is her resignation which has led her to choose this marriage in the first place. Like Mr. Bennet's, Charlotte's resignation grows out of despair; and it leads to a cynical view of human nature, human values, and the human condition. Austen does not ignore the difficulties of Charlotte's position. Charlotte's response, however, though understandable, is far from admirable. Anne Elliot would not consider even a Mr. Elliot (before she knows the truth), much less a Mr. Collins.

Another detached value which forms part of the code is perceptiveness. The detached person takes pride in his superior insight into both himself and others. He loves to analyze motives and to see through pretensions. He looks down upon others from the height of his understanding and has an ironical attitude toward people who lack self-awareness. These are recognizable traits both of a number of Austen's characters and of the author herself. There is a side of Jane Austen that enjoys the onlooker role and that revels in displays of wit and perception. Her irony serves not only her expansive needs for power, but also her detached needs for mental superiority. Her distrust of feeling is partly a manifestation of detachment. Because the detached person takes so much pride in his insight, he hates to be wrong; and nothing is more prejudicial to accurate perception than compulsive feelings. Austen's characters often discover their mistakes, much to their own chagrin. The author is aware of them all along, and through various techniques of irony she allows the reader to participate in her superiority. But Jane Austen is as blind as the rest of us when she is presenting a character whom she loves or with whom she profoundly identifies. These lapses of irony and insight provide the strongest possible evidence that she is not always, or even nearly always, detached.

Austen's celebration of perceptiveness is quite compatible with her perfectionistic trends, which also demand superior understanding; but it is in conflict with some of her self-effacing values. Detached perception can easily lead to amoral unconcern or even to cruelty. Mr. Bennet becomes callous toward his family, and his wit is a means of aggression. Elizabeth shows an awareness of the danger when she hopes that she " 'never ridicule[s] what is wise and good' " (I, xi). She feels guilty later on for having so " 'often disdained the generous candour of [Jane, and having] gratified [her] vanity, in useless or blameable distrust' " (II, xiii). There is a conflict in the code between generosity, one aspect of which is thinking well of others, and perceptiveness, which, more often than not, leads to disapproval or mockery.

195

What Jane Austen wants is to combine detached perception with strong principles and tenderness of heart. This is her intention, I believe, in *Northanger Abbey*. According to Marvin Mudrick, Henry Tilney "is the willfully ironic and detached spectator as no one except the author herself is in any other of Jane Austen's novels. Whenever he speaks, he speaks from the outside, to amuse, to parry, to lead on, to instruct, to humble; never plainly and straightforwardly, or unwarily, to reveal or engage himself" (p. 49). Austen certainly admires his wit, which resembles her own, just as she delights in the sallies of Mr. Bennet and Elizabeth. She is somewhat critical, however, of his ironic detachment: "Catherine feared . . . that he indulged himself a little too much with the foibles of others" (I, iii). Catherine is one of the good simple kind. Her approval of Henry is based, like that of the author, not upon "his manner," which "might sometimes surprize," but upon "his meaning," which is "always . . . just" (I, xiv).

Henry is not only a wit; he is also a good and sensible man. This is revealed by Catherine's attachment to him and even more by his appreciation of her, which is based upon a recognition of her virtues. His ironic description of Isabella Thorpe contains his actual appraisal of Catherine: " 'Open, candid, artless, guileless, with affections strong but simple, forming no pretensions, and knowing no disguise' " (II, x). He does not scorn her for her naive display of interest and admiration; he is charmed and reciprocates her affection. He takes an ironic view of Catherine's humors—her love of the old and her overheated imagination—but he is never ironic about her virtues; and he does speak plainly. He tells her that she is " 'superior in good-nature . . . to all the rest of the world' " (II, i) and that in her generous assessment of others she feels " 'what is most to the credit of human nature' " (II, x). His principles, like hers, are "steady" (II, xvi). He will not give Catherine up because his father wishes it, but neither will he marry without parental consent. Henry's irony is, like Catherine's overimaginativeness, a humor. Each character puts the excesses of the other in their place and brings out his fundamental goodness, which is alike in simple and complex.

The difficulty with this combination of perception with tenderness is that it is very schematic. Austen has given Henry an uncomplicated respect for simple goodness that is difficult to reconcile with his general sophistication. Elizabeth and Emma admire and sometimes even reverence the tenderheartedness and generosity of Jane and Harriet; but they never lose sight of their own mental superiority; and they would not think of marrying someone who was not their equal. Henry Tilney seems sacrificed to Jane Austen's thematic intentions. It is hard to believe that he will not soon be bored. *Northanger Abbey* is not a realistic novel, of course; and it is inappropriate to judge it as if it were. But it is one of Austen's most notable attempts to synthesize the values of perceptiveness and generosity; and her difficulty in doing it here is an indication of the tension between these values and a harbinger of her later struggles.

A final aspect of the detached solution toward which Austen has mixed feelings is withdrawal. Whereas the expansive person moves against and the self-effacing person moves toward people, the detached person handles a frustrating or threatening world by moving away from other people, both physically and emotionally. Fanny Price takes refuge in the solitude of the East room, in the vacuity of her hours with Lady Bertram, and in the quiet pleasures of reading and reflection. Sir Thomas invites few guests and makes of Mansfield "a sombre family-party" (II, iii). Anne Elliot defends herself against the indifference of her family and the shabby treatment she receives by becoming inwardly aloof from them. Mr. Bennet retires into his wit and his library, and Elizabeth turns to detached humor as a defense against situations which would be too painful if she were to take them seriously.

Austen is sympathetic toward the need of sensitive and intelligent people to move away from those who oppress them, and she herself seems to resort to humor to make life tolerable in a world composed largely of fools. Some forms of withdrawal are innocent enough, but others lead to irresponsibility and a betrayal of the code. Sir Thomas is too aloof from his family. He does not pay enough attention to his children's education, and he allows Fanny to be persecuted and his daughters to be spoiled by the pernicious Mrs. Norris. Lady Bertram, whom Professor Trilling seems strangely to admire, is even more of a moral nonentity than Mr. Bennet. And Elizabeth's education consists partly in accepting the pain, and along with it the responsibility, of being a member of her family.

4

As I have shown, Jane Austen's personality manifests all of the Horneyan trends. Her code contains a mixture of perfectionistic, detached, and self-effacing values; and she identifies herself at one point or another with components, at least, of all the solutions. Her own inner conflicts contribute, no doubt, to her remarkable understanding of a wide range of psychological types. Each of the solutions has its concomitant daydreams; and if we look at the dominating fantasies of each of her novels, we will see that they, too, display variety and conflict rather than singleness of vision. *Northanger Abbey* is a fantasy of the reconciliation of naive goodness with ironic detachment. *Sense and Sensibility* fantasizes the dangers of sensibility and the triumph of perfectionism. *Pride and Prejudice* is a wish fulfillment fantasy of the expansive solution, in which a recognition of the heroine's superiority brings wealth and grandeur. *Mansfield Park* fantasizes the vindication of self-effacing goodness and ennoblement through suffering and deprivation. *Emma* imagines the dangers of narcissism and the rewards of humility and perfection. *Persuasion* envisions the lifting of resignation and the achievement of ultimate gratification through goodness and rectitude. We have, then, fantasies which are predominantly perfectionistic, predominantly expansive, and predominantly self-effacing in *Sense and Sensibility, Pride and Prejudice,* and *Mansfield Park,* respectively, and fantasies which combine self-effacing and perfectionistic elements in *Emma* and *Persuasion.*

When Jane Austen's novels are considered in the order of their composition, there are some striking shifts of direction which make it difficult to understand her development and to generalize about her total personality. *Pride and Prejudice* is the only novel which embodies a predominantly expansive fantasy, and it is followed by the only novel in which the self-effacing solution is unremittingly glorified. *Mansfield Park* is followed by *Emma,* which celebrates the heroine's humiliation, but which also presents the fullest array of self-effacing humors characters. The novels which most closely resemble each other come from the beginning and the end of Austen's career. Elinor and Anne are more alike psychologically than are any other pair of complex characters.

Despite the difficulties, I shall attempt some generalizations. Jane Austen is, it seems to me, a predominantly perfectionistic person who takes great pride in her standards, her genius, and her rectitude. She also has strong self-effacing trends which manifest themselves in all of her novels and which sometimes become dominant. She admires purely self-effacing people for their generosity, tenderheartedness, and humility, and is somewhat defensive about her own deficiency in these qualities. Both her perfectionistic and her self-effacing trends lead her to recoil from the narcissistic and the arrogant-vindictive forms of the expansive solution. When these surface in her characters or in herself, she turns to the crushing of pride and other forms of suffering for an antidote. There are submerged aggressive drives within her, however, which manifest themselves in her satire, in her sympathy with the need for recognition, and in the real value which she gives to wealth and position. Detachment is the third strongest element in her personality. She takes great pride in her discernment, enjoys looking down upon others from the height of her understanding, and is sympathetic toward impulses of withdrawal and resignation. She is critical of detachment, however, when it leads to a violation of perfectionistic or self-effacing values. This personality structure is dynamic in nature. Jane Austen is constantly trying to achieve an equilibrium between opposing forces. She has a need to criticize each solution from the point of view of the others, and a strong movement in any one direction tends to activate the opposing trends.

If this analysis of Austen's authorial personality is combined with a knowledge of her life, it becomes possible to formulate a theory of her development. In *Sense and Sensibility* she articulates her standards and proclaims her maturity. This demonstration of her moral superiority satisfies her perfectionistic needs and releases the fantasy of power and recognition which is embodied in *Pride and Prejudice*. *Mansfield Park* is an almost penitential reaction in the opposite direction. It is severe upon worldly, expansive people, however charming they may be; and it affirms the importance of self-effacing goodness and humility. *Pride and Prejudice* is an expression of youthful self-confidence and girlish hopes and dreams. *Mansfield Park* is written from the perspective of frustrated middle age; it displays a strong need to glorify suffering and privation. Austen comes to terms with the hardships of her life by turning her submission into a source of moral grandeur. The writing of *Mansfield Park* satisfies her self-effacing shoulds and frees her from the anxiety generated by *Pride and Prejudice*. This, combined perhaps with her success as an author, allows her to return in *Emma* to her old posture of perfectionistic condescension. *Emma* is another criticism of the expansive solution and celebration of self-effacing virtues; but Austen does not seem to be as threatened by the first or as enamored of the second as she was in *Mansfield Park*. She reverts to her humorous treatment of simple self-effacing types, and she writes her only novel which is entirely free of villains. She is morally serious, but in the good-natured, tolerant manner of assured superiority.

In *Persuasion* the irony, the assurance, and the impersonality of *Emma* are gone; and Jane Austen is mourning for what she has missed in life. *Persuasion* is, like *Sense and Sensibility*, a fantasy of the recognition and reward of a perfectionistic heroine. It is in many ways a rewriting of the earlier novel from the perspective of a larger experience. Anne differs from Elinor principally in being older, in having stronger self-effacing trends, and in being more resigned. She is an Elinor who has endured a long period of frustration and who has learned that perfect rectitude, however consoling, is not enough for happiness. The novel clearly expresses a wish on Austen's part for a renewal of youthful hope and confidence and for the gratifications of love. The good society in this novel is more in keeping with the spirit of comedy than are the societies represented by Mansfield Park, Hartfield, or even Pemberley. Even at the end, these were all more or less closed worlds which embodied conservative values. The naval society represents devotion to duty, to be sure; but is is also characterized by gusto, spontaneity, and openness to experience. As a consequence, it is less safe. The effects of the Napoleonic Wars are more vividly present in *Persuasion* than in any of the other novels; but the characters seem able to confront their more turbulent world without undue anxiety. In this last of her novels, which she wrote while she was dying, Jane Austen seems to be emerging from embeddedness and to be embracing life.

Notes

Chapter I

1. *Anatomy of Criticism* (Princeton: Princeton University Press, 1957), p. 51; hereafter referred to in the text as *AC*.
2. Northrop Frye, "Myth, Fiction, and Displacement," in *Fables of Identity* (New York and Burlingame: Harcourt, Brace, & World, 1963), p. 36. The next quotation is from the same passage.
3. See *A Psychological Approach to Fiction: Studies in Thackeray, Stendhal, George Eliot, Dostoevsky, and Conrad* (Bloomington: Indiana University Press, 1974), Chapters 1 and 8.
4. "Character and Event in Fiction," *The Yale Review*, L (1960), 211.
5. New York: Oxford University Press, 1966.
6. Ithaca: Cornell University Press, 1965, Appendix I.
7. An exposition of the psychological theories which I shall use can be found in Chapter II, pp. 33-36 and pp. 39-44. Readers who wish to skip my discussion of *Mansfield Park* should read those pages before proceeding to any of the later chapters.
8. For a fuller discussion of the disparity between representation and interpretation, see *A Psychological Approach to Fiction*, Chapter 1. By representation I do not mean copying, but rather artistic selection for the purpose of creating a psychological portrait. Interpretation includes analysis and judgment.

Chapter II

1. Lionel Trilling, *The Opposing Self*, Viking Compass edition (New York: Viking Press, 1959), p. 213.
2. Riverside edition, ed. Reuben A. Brower (Boston: Houghton Mifflin, 1965) Book III, Chapter iii. Book and chapter references will hereafter be given in parentheses after the quotation. If no reference is given, the quotation is from the chapter last cited.

3. For the fullest analysis so far, see Avrom Fleishman, *A Reading of Mansfield Park* (Minneapolis: University of Minnesota Press, 1967), Chapter IV.
4. For a fuller account of Third Force psychology, see *A Psychological Approach to Fiction,* Chapter II.
5. Karen Horney, *Neurosis and Human Growth* (New York: Norton, 1950), p. 15. Hereafter cited as *NHG.*
6. Abraham Maslow, *Toward a Psychology of Being* (Princeton: Van Nostrand, 1962), pp. 3-4. Hereafter cited as *PB.*
7. There are several other needs which Maslow defines as basic, but which he does not integrate into his hierarchy of prepotency. They are the needs to know and to understand and the aesthetic needs. For a fuller discussion of each of the basic needs, see Maslow, *Motivation and Personality* (New York, Evanston, and London: Harper & Row, 1954), Chapter 5. This work will be cited hereafter as *MP.*
8. Carl Rogers, *On Becoming a Person* (Boston: Houghton Mifflin, 1961), p. 51.
9. *Metamorphosis* (New York: Basic Books, 1959), p. 151. Hereafter cited as *M.*
10. *New Ways in Psychoanalysis* (New York: Norton, 1939), p. 75.
11. *Our Inner Conflicts* (New York: Norton, 1945), p. 219. Hereafter cited as *OIC.*
12. *The Neurotic Personality of Our Time* (New York: Norton, 1936), p. 68. Hereafter cited as *NP.*

Chapter III

1. *The Rhetoric of Fiction* (Chicago: University of Chicago Press, 1961), p. 259.
2. Horney has written only a few pages about the narcissistic and the perfectionistic strategies *(NHG,* pp. 193-97). While they have helped me to understand Emma, my study of Emma has given me far more insight than Horney offers into the dynamics of these solutions.

Chapter V

1. For a fuller discussion of the psychology of the narrator, see George Graeber, "Comic, Thematic, and Mimetic Impulses in Jane Austen's *Persuasion,"* Diss., Michigan State University, 1977, Chapter IV. Graeber uses Frye and Horney, as I do; but he makes a number of points which I do not, he disagrees with me on some issues, and he amplifies many ideas which have been treated briefly here.

Chapter VI

1. For another, though much briefer, analysis of an authorial personality, see my essay on Thomas Hardy in *The Victorian Experience,* ed. Richard A. Levine (Athens, Ohio: Ohio University Press, 1976), pp. 203-37. This essay also explores the ways in which the psychology of the reader affects his responses to an author.
2. *The Works of Jane Austen,* Vol. VI (Minor Works), ed. R. W. Chapman (London: Oxford University Press, 1954), p. 78. All quotations from the *Juvenilia* are from this volume. Page numbers will hereafter be given in the text.
3. Jane Austen began to conceive of such characters as early as "Lesley Castle" *(Volume the Second).* Louisa Burton "was naturally ill-tempered and Cunning; but

she had been taught to disguise her real Disposition, under the appearance of insinuating sweetness. . . . By dint of Perseverance and Application, she had at length so thoroughly disguised her natural disposition under the mask of Innocence and Softness, as to impose upon every one who had not by a long and constant intimacy with her discovered her real Character" (pp. 117-18).

4. Quotations in this paragraph are from *Our Inner Conflicts*, pp. 63-65.
5. *The Works of Jane Austen*, Vol. VI, p. 248. Page numbers will hereafter be given in the text.
6. Quotations in this paragraph and the next are from *Neurosis and Human Growth*, pp. 196-97.
7. Quotations in this paragraph are from *Jane Austen: Irony as Defense and Discovery* (Princeton: Princeton University Press, 1952), pp. 1 and 91.
8. Alistair Duckworth, *The Improvement of the Estate: A Study of Jane Austen's Novels* (Baltimore: The Johns Hopkins Press, 1971), p. 28.
9. C. S. Lewis, "A Note on Jane Austen," in *Jane Austen: A Collection of Critical Essays*, ed. Ian Watt (Englewood Cliffs, N. J.: Prentice Hall, 1963), p. 33.
10. Lionel Trilling, *The Opposing Self*, p. 206.
11. For a novel which celebrates the virtues of resignation, see Thomas Hardy's *The Mayor of Casterbridge*.

Index

205

Index

Conflict
—between form and mimesis, 11, 13-14, 18-20; in *Emma*, 64-65, 93; in *Mansfield Park*, 22-23, 32, 62; in *Persuasion*, 167
—between form and theme, 16-17
—between reader's interpretation and author's, 20-21; in *Emma*, 72-73, 95; in *Mansfield Park*, 23, 49, 61-63; in *Pride and Prejudice*, 122
—between theme and mimesis, 16-17, 20-21; in *Emma*, 64-65, 72-73, 93; in *Mansfield Park*, 22-23, 32-33, 36-37, 49, 61-63; in *Persuasion*, 158; in *Pride and Prejudice*, 97-98, 132-33, 134, 136, 139
—in reader's expectations, 19-20
—within JA's authorial personality, 10, 170, 176, 195-96, 198-201
—within JA's code, 193-94, 195-96, 198
Crawford, Henry, 26, 30-31, 53-57 passim, 62, 177, 181

Darcy, Fitzwilliam, 98-99, 101, 104-5, 107, 112, 132, 177, 181
—psychological analysis of, 136-39
Dashwood, Elinor, 15, 172, 182, 200
—psychological anaylsis of, 184-87, 193-94
Dashwood, Marianne, 15, 29, 172, 187-88
Despised self, 44
Detached solution, 40-41, 43, 204 n.11
—authorial personality's, 191-93, 195, 199
—Anne Elliot's, 156-57, 160, 163-65, 193-94, 197
—Charlotte Lucas's, 113-14, 194
—Elinor Dashwood's, 193-94
—Elizabeth Bennet's, 119-21, 128, 197
—Emma Woodhouse's, 83-84
—Fanny Price's, 47-48, 197
—Henry Tilney's, 196-97
—JA's attitude toward, 191-98, 199-200
—Mr. Bennet's, 114-18, 197
—Sir Thomas Bertram's, 197-98
Development, JA's, 198-201
Displacement
—Frye's theory of, 14
—in JA's novels, 15-16
Dostoevsky, Fyodor, 170

Elliot, Anne, 10, 15, 17, 172-74, 182, 188, 194-95, 197, 200-201
—as comic heroine, 140-41, 143-47
—as illustrative character, 141-42, 147-55 passim
—psychological analysis of, 142-43, 155-67, 193-95
Elliot, Mr., 146, 174, 177
Embeddedness, 35-36
—of Fanny Price, 38-39
—JA emerging from, 201
—of Mr. Woodhouse, 81
Emma, 10, 16, 64-95, 177, 190, 200
—dominating fantasy of, 198
—formal analysis of, 65-68
—psychological analysis of, 73-95
—thematic analysis of, 68-71
"Evelyn," 189-90
Expansive solution. *See* Aggressive solution

Fantasies, dominating, of JA's novels, 198-201
Ferrars, Edward, 173, 186-87
Form
—comic, in JA's novels, 14-17. *See also* Comic structure
—and mimesis, 11, 13-14, 18-20
—and theme, 15-16
Forster, E.M., 8
"Frederick & Elfrida," 188-89
Freud, Sigmund, 14
Frye, Northrop, 9
—on comic structure, 14-16, 66, 99, 100, 143, 144-45
—on displacement, 14
—on tension between myth and mimesis, 13-14

Graeber, George, 203 n.1

Harding, D. W., 10
Harvey, W. J., 18
Horney, Karen, 9, 11, 33-36, 39-44

Idealized image, 44

Jane Austen: Irony as Defense and Discovery, 10
Juvenilia, 171, 175, 188

Index

*Bernard J. Paris is a professor of English and com-
parative literature at Michigan State University,
East Lansing, Michigan. He received his A.B. (1952)
and his Ph.D. (1959) from
The Johns Hopkins University.*

*The manuscript was edited by Patricia L. Cornett.
The book was designed by Don Ross. The typeface
for the text is Times Roman, designed under the
supervision of Stanley Morison about 1932. The
display face is Caslon 540, based on an original
design by William Caslon about 1720.*

*The text is printed on Booktext Natural paper and the
book is bound in Joanna Mills' Oxford cloth
(spine) and Joanna Mills' Linson cloth (sides).
Manufactured in the United States of America.*